THE RAIN OR SHINE ACTIVITY BOOK

Fun Things to Make and Do

by Joanna Cole and
Stephanie Calmenson

illustrated by Alan Tiegreen

MORROW JUNIOR BOOKS • NEW YORK

Published by Morrow Junior Books
a division of William Morrow and Company, Inc.
1350 Avenue of the Americas, New York, NY 10019

Printed in the United States of America.

1 2 3 4 5 6 7 8 9 10

Library of Congress Cataloging-in-Publication Data
Cole, Joanna.
The rain or shine activity book/by Joanna Cole and Stephanie Calmenson; illustrated by Alan Tiegreen.
p. cm.
Summary: Gives directions for games and amusements of all kinds, including riddles, tongue-twisters, card games, street rhymes, brainteasers, and fun with string.
ISBN 0-688-12131-4
1. Amusements—Juvenile literature.   2. Games—Juvenile literature.   3. Creative activities and seat work—Juvenile literature.   4. Rhyming games—Juvenile literature.   [1. Amusements.   2. Games.   3. Handicraft.]   I. Calmenson, Stephanie.   II. Tiegreen, Alan, ill.   III. Title.   GV1229.C55 1997
793—DC21   96-37756   CIP AC

CONTENTS

INTRODUCTION

Pick a day. Any day.

It could be rainy or sunny, a school day or a vacation day, a day with friends or a day alone. No matter what kind of day it is, you're going to want to have some fun, right? That's what we thought.

So we've collected activities for any day you can think of. We've got riddles, rhymes, tongue twisters, crafts, paper games, street games, and magic tricks. You'll find over ninety activities in this book. So go ahead, pick one. And have some fun.

RIDDLES

ABOUT RIDDLES

**I have an apple I cannot cut,
A blanket I cannot fold,
And so much money I cannot count it.**

This is a riddle that was told long, long ago. The first riddles, say folklorists, go far back in human history. They were not necessarily funny. Rather, they were a way of looking at the world. They showed how two things that seem different on the surface are actually alike in some way. Many were about nature and the universe, and often they were more like poems than jokes.

The answer to the riddle above is: the moon, which is round like an apple; the sky, which is large and flat like a blanket; and the stars, which are scattered through the heavens like sparkling coins.

Other old riddles were matters of life and death. In the mythology of ancient Greece, a dragonlike creature called the Sphinx sat outside the city of Thebes and asked this riddle of everyone who passed:

**What walks on four legs in the morning,
two legs at noon, and three legs at night?**

Those who couldn't answer were killed by the Sphinx. Finally a man named Oedipus solved the riddle and destroyed the Sphinx. The answer he gave was: man, who crawls on all fours as a baby, walks on two feet as a man, and uses a cane in old age.

Riddles have changed a lot over the years. Now they are told mostly to amuse. The humor comes from playing with language, from taking advantage of the fact that one word often has two or more meanings. Your life may never depend on knowing the answers to the riddles in this book, but we hope they'll make you laugh.

Here is a riddle we'd like to close with:

Why did the pig keep turning around when he read this introduction?

He was looking for the end.

And here it is. . .

The End

WHAT DO YOU CALL A BABY WHALE?

Here are some silly ways to describe things.

What do you call two bananas?

A pair of slippers.

What do you call a sick alligator?

An illigator.

What do you call a baby whale?

A little squirt.

What do you call a bee who hums very quietly?
A mumblebee.

What do you call a pony with a sore throat?
A little hoarse.

What do you call a freight train loaded with bubble gum?
A chew-chew train.

What do you call someone who carries an encyclopedia in his pocket?
Smarty-pants.

MORE ANIMAL RIDDLES

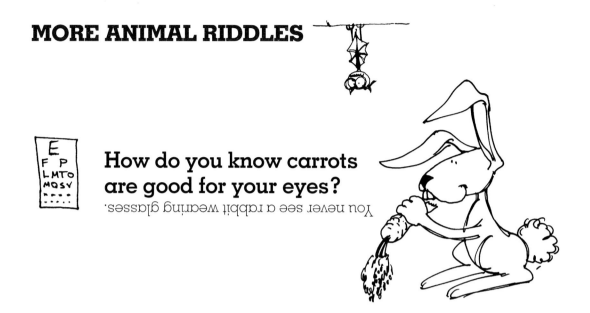

How do you know carrots are good for your eyes?

You never see a rabbit wearing glasses.

What is the best way to catch a squirrel?

Climb up a tree and act like a nut.

Why is it hard to talk with a goat around?

He keeps butting in.

Why don't ducks tell jokes while they're flying?

They might quack up.

Why does a mother kangaroo hope it doesn't rain?

She hates it when the children have to play inside.

What did the boy octopus say to the girl octopus?

I want to hold your hand, hand, hand, hand, hand, hand, hand, hand.

There were ten cats in a boat and one jumped out. How many were left?

None. They were copycats.

WHAT BOW CAN'T BE TIED?
Things are not always what they seem.

What kind of coat won't keep you warm?

A coat of paint.

What pool is no good for swimming?

A car pool.

What bow can't be tied?

A rainbow.

Which pen won't write?

A pigpen.

WHAT DID DELAWARE?

Is geography funny? Try these riddles and see.

What did Delaware?

She wore her New Jersey.

What did Idaho?

She hoed her Maryland.

What did Tennessee?

She saw what Arkansas.

What state has four eyes but can't see?

Mississippi.

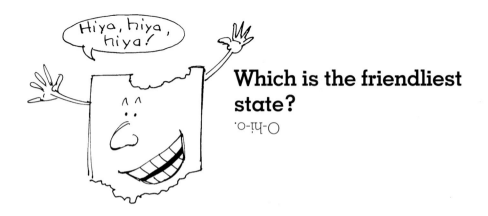

Hiya, hiya, hiya!

Which is the friendliest state?

O-hi-o.

If the green house is on the right side of the road and the red house is on the left side of the road, where is the white house?

In Washington, D.C.

Who should you call when you find Chicago, Ill?

Baltimore, MD.

Can you name the capital of every state in the union in less than fifteen seconds?

Yes, Washington, D.C.

Where do cows go on vacation?

Moo York.

LETTER RIDDLES

What word begins with *E*, ends with *E*, and sounds as if it has only one letter in it?

Eye (I).

Spell *we* using two letters other than *W* or *E*.

U and I.

What five-letter word has six left when you take away two letters?

Sixty.

Why is *B* such a hot letter?

It makes oil boil.

Why is honey so scarce in Boston?
Because there is only one B in Boston.

How can you make a witch scratch?
Take away her W.

What letters can climb a wall?
I-V (ivy).

Which are the coldest two letters?
I-C (icy).

WHAT COLOR WAS WASHINGTON'S WHITE HORSE?

Watch out for these tricky riddles!

Antidisestablishmentarianism is the longest word in the English language. How do you spell it?

I-T.

How much dirt is in a hole
six feet long by thirteen feet wide?

None. A hole is empty.

**Which weighs more: a pound
of lead or a pound of feathers?**

They both weigh a pound.

What color was Washington's white horse?

White.

How many animals did Moses take on the ark?

Moses didn't take any animals on the ark. Noah did.

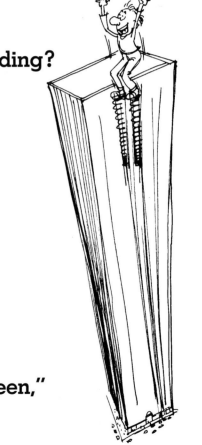

Who can jump higher than a tall building?

Anyone can. Tall buildings can't jump.

If a rooster laid a white egg and a brown egg, what kinds of chicks would hatch?

None. Roosters don't lay eggs.

Do you say, "Eight and seven *is* thirteen," or "Eight and seven *are* thirteen"?

Neither. Eight and seven equal fifteen.

TONGUE TWISTERS

GETTING STARTED

Warm up your tongue with these twisters.

Nat's knapsack strap snapped.

Sam's sock shop stocks short spotted socks.

Rubber baby buggy bumpers.

Andy ran to the Andes from the Indies in his undies.

Shirley sewed Sly's shirt shut.

Pick up six pick-up sticks quickly.

SHEEPISH SHAYINGS...
ER, WE MEAN SHEEPISH SAYINGS

Six sick sheep.
The sixth sick sheep is the sheik's sixth sheep.

Sheep shouldn't sleep in a shack.
Sheep should sleep in a shed.

Say, does this sheet shop serve sheep, sir?

Sam shaved seven shy sheep.
Seven shaved sheep shivered shyly.

SHORT TAKES

Say these two-word twisters three times fast.
They may be short, but they're not easy.

Preshrunk shirts.

Lemon liniment.

Truly rural.

Mixed biscuits.

Soldiers' shoulders.

Peggy Babcock.

Greek grapes.

Aluminum linoleum.

OVER AND OVER AND OVER

These twisters repeat one word many times.
What makes them extra-fun is that the same
word has two meanings.

I have a can opener that can open any can that any can
opener that can open any can can open. If you will give
me a can that any can opener that can open any can can
open, I will open that can that any can opener that can
open any can can open with my can opener that can
open any can that any can opener that can open any can
can open.

I thought a thought.
But the thought I thought
wasn't the thought
I thought I thought.
If the thought I thought
I thought had been
the thought I thought,
I wouldn't have
thought so much.

Of all the felt I ever felt, I never felt
a piece of felt that felt the same
as that felt felt when I first felt felt.

IMPRESS YOUR FRIENDS

Betty Botter bought some butter.
"But," she said, "the butter's bitter.
If I put it in my batter,
It will make my batter bitter,
But a bit of better butter,
That would make my batter better."
So she bought a bit of butter
Better than her bitter butter,
And she put it in her batter,
And the batter was not bitter.
So t'was better Betty Botter
Bought a bit of better butter.

Mr. See owned a saw.
And Mr. Soar owned a seesaw.
Now See's saw sawed Soar's seesaw
Before Soar saw See,
Which made Soar sore.
Had Soar seen See's saw
Before See sawed Soar's seesaw,
See's saw would not have sawed
Soar's seesaw.
So See's saw sawed Soar's seesaw,
But it was sad to see Soar so sore
Just because See's saw sawed Soar's seesaw.

ALPHABET GAME

You can play this game by yourself, simply making up a twister for each letter of the alphabet. For more players, the first player must make up a tongue twister for the letter *A*. The next player makes up one for *B*, and so on in turn.

Tips for making twisters: Think of sounds that confuse the tongue—such as *th* and *thr*, as in three thin thumbs; *f*, *fr*, and *fl*, as in fat flying frogs; or *s* and *sh*, as in she sells seashells.

A **Ask after Asta's asthma.**

B **Bessie bought Beth's beef broth.**

C **Clowns crown crabs and clams.**

D Ducks, don't drive, dive!

E Ethel's elegant elephant'll elevate Ethel.

...and so on, until *Z*.

TWISTERS

A tutor who tooted a flute
Tried to tutor two tooters to toot.
Said the two to their tutor,
"Is it harder to toot or
To tutor two tooters to toot?"

SAY-IT-AGAIN GAME

For two or more players.

Each player takes a turn saying a twister over and over again until he or she makes a mistake. The player who repeats the twister the most times is the winner.

You can use any tongue twister in this book, but the ones that follow are especially hard to say more than once.

Which wristwatch is the Swiss wristwatch?

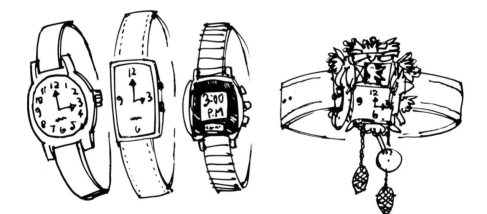

Red leather, yellow leather.

Double bubble gum bubbles double.

CARD GAMES

CRAZY EIGHTS
You'll love the eights
in this game—they're wild!

Number of players: Three or more
Object of game: To get rid of all your cards

1. Shuffle and deal seven cards to each player. Place the deck face down in the middle of the table. This is the pick-up pile. Turn one card face up next to the pile. This is the throw-away pile.

2. Players hold their cards in a fan and arrange them by suits—the Hearts together, the Clubs together, and so on.

3. The first player has to lay a card on top of the face-up card. This card has to be of the *same suit*—a Club on a Club, a Heart on a Heart, and so on.

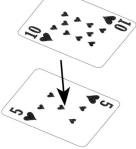

4. If you want to change suits, you can lay down a card of the *same number*—a 10 of Spades on a 10 of Hearts, for example. The next player must then put down a card of the new suit.

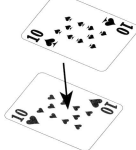

5. Eights are "wild"—that is, you may put down an 8 anytime and call out *any suit you wish*. It does not have to be the suit of the 8.

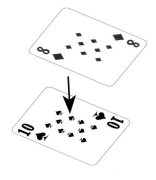

6. **If you have no matching cards and no 8's, you must draw cards from the pick-up pile until you find one you can lay down.**

7. **When the pick-up pile runs out, turn the throw-away pile face down to make a new one. (Don't forget to shuffle it!)**

8. **The first player to lay down all her cards is the winner.**

Helpful hints: Notice which suits have been put down. For example, if a lot of Diamonds have been played and you still have Diamonds in your hand, try to change the suit to Diamonds.

Eights are very valuable. Don't waste them. Use 8's to stop someone who is close to winning, or to change the suit if that will help you win.

For a quicker, easier game, deal out only five cards to each player.

ACES UP
Get the Aces up and the rest of the cards will follow.

Number of players: One—it's a solitaire game.
Object of game: To get all the cards into four piles—one pile for each suit—in the "Places for Aces"

SETTING UP THE GAME

♣ Lay out a row of seven
  cards *face down*. Leave
  room above for four
  "Places for Aces"

        seven cards

♣ Put another card face down
  on top of each card.

        fourteen cards

♣ Then lay down another row. This time do it *face up*.
  Lay the rest of the pack
  on the table face down.
  This is your stockpile.
  Now you are ready
  to play.

        twenty-one cards

— *40* —

THE PLACES FOR ACES

1. Look at the face-up cards. If you see any Aces, move them up to the Places for Aces. If any face-down cards are uncovered, turn them over.

2. Look at the cards again. If you see any 2's that match the Aces, move them up on top of the Aces. The 2 of Hearts goes on the Ace of Hearts, the 2 of Clubs goes on the Ace of Clubs, and so on. Then look for 3's, 4's, and so on. If you find any, move them up, too.

You've moved up the Ace of Spades. Turn over the card underneath. When you find the 2 of Spades, move it up on top of the Ace.

BUILDING LADDERS

3. If you don't see any more cards to move up, look at your seven face-up cards again. You want to build "ladders" of cards that go down from the original seven. These ladders will have cards going from higher numbers to lower numbers. You always put a red card on a black card and a black card on a red card.

    The suits don't matter here—only the colors and numbers are important. For example, a red 5 can be put only on a black 6. Then you can pick up the 5 and the 6 together and put them on a red 7.

Whenever you turn over a card that belongs in an Ace pile, move it up. Don't forget to turn over the card underneath.

MOVING LADDERS

4. You have to move the whole ladder together. You cannot move just part of a ladder, and you cannot pull a card from the middle of the ladder. There is *one* card you *can* move by itself—the last card on the ladder. You can move it to another ladder, another pile, or to the Places for Aces.

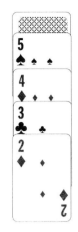

TURNING THE STOCKPILE

5. When no more cards can be moved, turn over the first three cards in your stockpile and lay them in a pile on the table in front of you. Look at all the cards on the table. Can you put the top card on the Places for Aces or on one of your ladders?

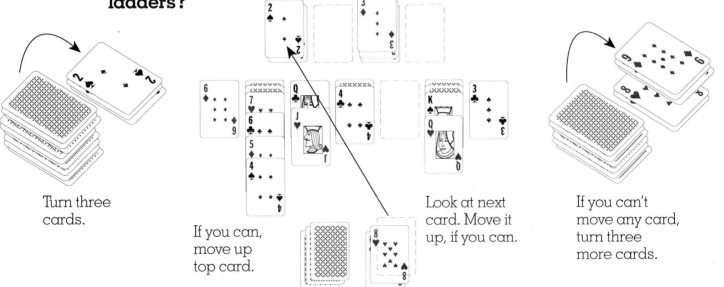

Turn three cards.

If you can, move up top card.

Look at next card. Move it up, if you can.

If you can't move any card, turn three more cards.

6. Keep going through the stockpile three cards at a time. When you finish, turn the pile over and start again.

7. What happens when one of the seven piles becomes empty? You may put a King—by itself, or with its ladder—on the empty spot. If there is no King on the table, wait until one shows up as you play.

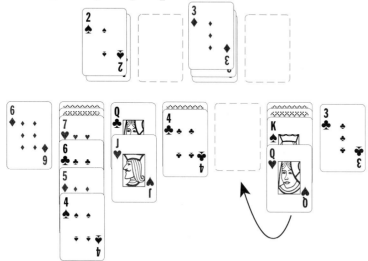

Is there an empty spot? Move a King there—by itself or with its ladder.

8. If you move all the cards up to the Ace piles, you won! However, if the time comes when you keep going through the pack and find no more cards to move, the game is over, and you lost. Pick up all the cards, shuffle them, and set up for another game!

I won!

PLAYING ACES UP WITH TWO PLAYERS

1. Two players sit at a table across from each other. Each player has her own deck of fifty-two cards. The backs of the cards must have different colors or patterns so you can tell them apart.

2. Each player sets up her own layout, the same as in one-player Aces Up. Players leave room in the middle of the table for *eight* Places for Aces—four Aces from each deck.

3. Each player follows the rules for one-player Aces Up. The only difference is that both players may put cards up on all eight Aces. It does not matter which Aces belong to which deck.

4. When no more cards can be moved by either player, the game ends. Players turn over the Ace piles and separate their cards from their opponent's cards. Whoever has the most cards in the Places for Aces is the winner.

 ### *SNAP*

Watch for cards that match,
then be the first to say, "Snap!"

Number of players: Good for two
Object of game: To get all the cards

1. Shuffle and deal out all the cards—including the Jokers.

2. Each player holds his pack face down.

3. Together the players say, "One, two, three." On the word *three,* the players quickly lay their top cards face up in the middle of the table.

4. If the cards do *not* match, the players repeat, "One, two, three" and lay down the next card.

5. If the cards match—two Kings, two 10's, two Aces—the first player to call out "Snap!" takes the cards.

She said "Snap" first. She takes the cards.

6. If both players call "Snap" at the same time, neither player takes the cards.

7. If you say "Snap" by mistake, you have to give one card to every player.

8. If one of the Jokers turns up, it's as good as a match. Again, the first player to call out "Snap!" takes the cards.

9. The player who gets all the cards is the winner.

SLAPJACK

You have to be fast to play this game.
When you see a Jack—slap it!

Number of players: Two to six
Object of game: To get all the cards

1. Shuffle and deal out all the cards.

2. Each player puts his pack face down on the table in front of him.

3. The first player *quickly* puts his top card face up in the center of the table. When putting down cards, turn them fast and *do not peek!*

4. The next player puts his card face up on top of the first card, and so on.

Turn the cards over with one hand. Use the *other* hand to slap.

5. When a Jack is turned over, all the players try to slap their hand on it. The first player to slap the Jack wins the pile.

6. The next player then puts a new card out, and the game goes on as before.

7. If a player runs out of cards, he sits without playing until a Jack comes up. Then he tries to slap the Jack and get back in the game.

8. The winner is the one who ends up with all the cards.

MY SHIP SAILS

In this game, you win when all your cards
are the same suit.

Number of players: Four or more
Object of game: To get any seven cards of the same suit, for example:

| seven Hearts | seven Diamonds | seven Clubs | seven Spades |

♣ Pay attention to suits in this game.

1. Shuffle and deal seven cards to each player. Put the rest of
   the deck aside. You will not need it.

2. Hold your cards in a fan. Arrange them by suit—put all the
   Hearts together, all the Clubs together, and so on. Don't
   worry if you don't have all the suits.

3. Each player passes one card face down to the player on his left.

4. When all the cards have been passed, everyone picks his card up at the same time. Each player puts the new card in his hand next to others of the same suit.

5. Then everyone passes a card again.

6. The game goes on until one player gets seven cards of the same suit. That player calls out, "My ship sails!" He is the winner.

HAND-CLAPPING RHYMES

To do a hand-clapping rhyme, face your partner, clap your hands in a special pattern, and say or sing the rhyme. The basic pattern goes like this: clap your own hands together; clap both your hands against your partner's hands; clap your own hands again; clap your partner's right hand with your right hand; clap your own hands together; and clap your partner's left hand with your left hand.

You can make the pattern more interesting by slapping your thighs, snapping your fingers, crossing your hands over your heart, or clapping the backs of your partner's hands with the backs of yours. Then speed up the clapping and see how fast you can go!

My boyfriend's name is Jello.
He comes from Monticello.
With three fat toes
And a dimple on his nose,
And that's the way my story goes.

As I went up the apple tree,
All the apples fell on me.
Bake a pudding, bake a pie,
Did you ever tell a lie?
Yes, you did, you know you did,
You broke your mother's teapot lid.

I am a pretty little Dutch girl,
As pretty as pretty can be.
And all the boys around the block
Are crazy over me, me, me.
I L-O-V-E, love you,
All the T-I-M-E, time.
I K-I-S-S, kiss you,
Please be M-I-N-E, mine, mine, mine.

Miss Lucy had a baby.
She named him Tiny Tim.
She put him in the bathtub
To see if he could swim.

He drank up all the water.
He ate up all the soap.
He tried to eat the bathtub,
But it wouldn't go down his throat.

Miss Lucy called the doctor.
Miss Lucy called the nurse.
Miss Lucy called the lady
With the alligator purse.

In walked the doctor,
In walked the nurse,
In walked the lady
With the alligator purse.

Miss Mary Mack, Mack, Mack,
All dressed in black, black, black,
With silver buttons, buttons, buttons,
All down her back, back, back.
She went upstairs to make her bed,
She made a mistake and bumped her head;
She went downstairs to wash the dishes,
She made a mistake and washed her wishes;
She went outside to hang her clothes,
She made a mistake and hung her nose.

Bo-bo-skee,
Watten-tatten,
Ah-ah,
Ah-ah,
Boom, boom, boom.
Eeny meeny,
Watten-tatten,
Bo-bo-skee,
Watten-tatten.
One slice,
Two slice,
Three slice,
Freeze!

(On the word "freeze," both players hold still; the
first to move or blink loses the contest.)

I met my boyfriend at the candy store.
He bought me candy,
He bought me cake,
He brought me home
With a bellyache.
Grandma, Grandma, I feel sick.
Call the doctor, quick, quick, quick.
Doctor, Doctor, will I die?
Close your eyes and count to five.
One, two, three, four, five.
I'm alive!

BALL-BOUNCING RHYMES

When you first learn to bounce a ball, it's a challenge to bounce it even a few times without missing. But pretty soon, that's too easy. Then it's fun to add some ball-bouncing rhymes. You bounce the ball in time to the rhythm, and you do stunts as you go. You usually turn your leg over the ball on the last word in each line. For variety, you can turn your *other* leg over, bounce the ball against a wall, clap your hands, or turn your whole body around between bounces. Sometimes you have to make up part of the rhyme yourself, so your brain has to work as you bounce.

Bouncie, bouncie, ballie.
My sister's name is Paulie.
I gave her a slap,
She paid me back,
Bouncie, bouncie, ballie.

Number one, touch your tongue.
Number two, touch your shoe.
Number three, touch your knee.
Number four, touch the floor.
Number five, learn to jive.
Number six, pick up sticks.
Number seven, go to heaven.
Number eight, shut the gate.
Number nine, touch your spine.
Number ten, do it all again!

(Act out the rhyme as you bounce.)

"A, My Name Is Alice" is a popular alphabet rhyme. Use the names, places, and things given here, or make up your own.

Bounce the ball on each word and turn your leg over the ball only on those words that begin with the letter that starts the verse. For example, in the first verse, turn on "A," "Alice," "And," "Al," "Alabama," "And," and "apples."

A, my name is Alice,
And my husband's name is Al.
We come from Alabama,
And we sell apples.

B, my name is Barbara,
And my husband's name is Bob.
We come from Boston,
And we sell beans.

C, my name is Carol,
And my husband's name is Carl.
We come from Chicago,
And we sell carts.

D, my name is Donna,
And my husband's name is Dave.
We come from Denver,
And we sell doughnuts.

E, my name is Ellen,
And my husband's name is Ed.
We come from Evanston,
And we sell eggs.

F, my name is Frances,
And my husband's name is Frank.
We come from Florida,
And we sell frankfurters.

G, my name is Gloria,
And my husband's name is Gus.
We come from Georgia,
And we sell gum.

H, my name is Harriet,
And my husband's name is Hank.
We come from Hohokus,
And we sell hoops.

I, my name is Ida,
And my husband's name is Irv.
We come from Indiana,
And we sell ice cream.

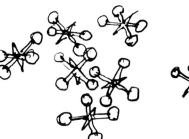

J, my name is Janet,
And my husband's name is John.
We come from Jamaica,
And we sell jacks.   and continue through the alphabet . . .

COUNTING-OUT RHYMES

When you are playing a game like tag or hide-and-seek, how do you pick who will be "It"? Use a counting-out rhyme.

Usually the players stand in a circle and the counter points to each person in turn for every word of the rhyme. The person on the last word goes out, and the counting starts over. Whoever is left at the end is "It."

Monkey, monkey, bottle of pop,
On which monkey do we stop?
One, two, three,
Out goes *he.*

Eena, meena, dippa deena,
Delia, dahlia, dominee,
Hatcha, patcha, dominatcha,
Hi, pon, tuss, *out.*

Eeny, meeny, figgledy fig,
Delia, dahlia, dominig,
Ozy, pozy, doma-nozy,
Tee, tau, tut.
Uggledy buggledy boo
Out goes *you!*

Eeny, meeny, miney, mo.
Catch a tiger by the toe.
If he hollers, let him go.
My mother says to pick this one,
And out goes Y-O-*U.*

COUNTING OUT WITH QUESTIONS AND ANSWERS

These counting-out rhymes all ask a question. If the counter points to you on the last word of the question, you must answer. Then the counter continues the rhyme. A different person will go out, depending on the answer given. (The answers shown here are just examples. You can answer any way you like.)

Engine, engine number nine
Running on Chicago line.
If the train should jump the track,
Do you want your money back?
  "Yes."
Y-E-S spells yes and you are not *It*.

Words that are printed this way— "Yes"
—are sample answers to the questions.

All around the butter dish,
One, two, three.
If you want a pretty girl,
Just pick me.
Blow the bugles,
Beat the drums.
Tell me when your birthday comes.
 "July tenth."
J-U-L-Y. One, two, three, four, five,
six, seven, eight, nine, *ten*.

Each, peach, pear, plum.
When does your birthday come?
 "April fourth."
A-P-R-I-L. One, two, three, *four*.

JUMP-ROPE RHYMES

STRAIGHT JUMPING

Skilled jumpers can do all sorts of fancy tricks and stunts, but often they prefer just plain jumping—with a good rhyme to keep the rhythm going. Here are some favorite rhymes.

—————————— △ ▽ △ ——————————

I went upstairs to make my bed.
I made a mistake and bumped my head.
I went downstairs to milk my cow.
I made a mistake and milked the sow.
I went in the kitchen to bake a pie.
I made a mistake and baked a fly.

Standing on the corner
Chewing bubble gum.
Along came a beggar
And asked me for some.

Standing at the bar
Smoking a cigar.
Laughing at the donkey
Ha—ha—har!

Tomatoes, lettuce, carrots, peas.
Mother said you have to eat a lot of these.

Ice cream, a penny a lump.
The more you eat—the more you jump!

As I was walking near the lake,
I met a little rattlesnake.
He ate so much of jelly-cake,
It made his little belly ache.

Postman, postman, do your duty.
Send this letter to an American beauty.
Don't you stop and don't delay.
Get it to her right away.

Johnny gave me apples,
Johnny gave me pears,
Johnny gave me fifty cents
And kissed me on the stairs.
I'd rather wash the dishes,
I'd rather scrub the floor,
I'd rather kiss the iceman
Behind the kitchen door.

HOW MANY?

It's a challenge to see how many times you can jump without missing. Here are rhymes for counting the number.

—————————△ ▽ △—————————

Chickety, chickety, chop.
How many times before I stop?
One, two, three, four, five, etc.

Candy, candy in the dish.
How many pieces do you wish?
One, two, three, four, five . . .

My mother made a chocolate cake.
How many eggs did it take?
One, two, three, four, five . . .

My little sister dressed in pink
Washed all the dishes in the sink.
How many dishes did she break?
One, two, three, four, five . . .

Cinderella dressed in red
Went downstairs to bake some bread.
How many loaves did she bake?
One, two, three, four, five . . .

Cinderella dressed in green
Went upstairs to eat ice cream.
How many spoonfuls did she eat?
One, two, three, four, five . . .

Cinderella dressed in blue
Went outside to tie her shoe.
How many seconds did it take?
One, two, three, four, five . . .

ACTIONS

Can you reach down and touch the ground
while jumping? These rhymes ask you to do
all kinds of things without missing a beat.

———————— △ ▽ △ ————————

I'm a little Dutch girl
Dressed in blue.
Here are the things
I like to do:
Salute to the captain,
Bow to the queen,
Turn my back
on the submarine.
I can do the tap dance,
I can do the split,
I can do the holka polka
Just like this.

Spanish dancer, do the split.
Spanish dancer, give a kick.
Spanish dancer, turn around.
Spanish dancer, get out of town.

(On the last line, the jumper runs out.)

Teddy bear, teddy bear,
Turn around.
Teddy bear, teddy bear,
Touch the ground.
Teddy bear, teddy bear,
Show your shoe.
Teddy bear, teddy bear,
That will do.
Teddy bear, teddy bear,
Go upstairs.
Teddy bear, teddy bear,
Say your prayers.
Teddy bear, teddy bear,
Turn out the light.
Teddy bear, teddy bear,
Say good night.

Apple on a stick,
Five cents a lick.
Every time I turn around
It makes me sick.

NOW'S THE TIME TO MISS

When the enders chant a rhyme about missing, they may speed up and try to make the jumper trip. Or the jumper herself may miss on purpose. She can choose to step on the rope, put a foot on either side of it, stand still, or just run out.

——————————△ ▽ △——————————

Andy, Mandy,
Sugar candy,
Now's the time to *miss!*

Jump rope, jump rope,
Will I miss?
Jump rope, jump rope,
Just watch this!

Miss, miss, little miss, miss.
When she misses, she misses like this.

I know a woman
And her name is Miss.
And all of a sudden
She goes like—this.

I know a man, his name is Mister.
He knows a lady, and her name is MISS.

Little Miss Pinky, dressed in blue,
Died last night at half-past two.
Before she died, she told me this,
"Let the jump rope miss like this."

YES, NO, MAYBE SO . . .

Some rhymes ask a question followed by a list of possible answers. The choice may be a simple "yes, no, yes, no," or it may be a list of colors, houses, or numbers. The word you happen to miss on is the answer.

───────────△ ▽ △───────────

My ma and your ma were
    hanging out the clothes.
My ma gave your ma
    a punch in the nose.
Did it hurt her?
Yes, no, maybe so, yes, no, maybe so . . .

My little girl, dressed in blue,
Died last night at half-past two.
Did she go up or down?
Up, down, up, down, up, down . . .

What shall I name my little pup?
I'll have to think a good one up.
A, B, C, D, E, F, G . . .

(When the jumper misses, she makes up a name
beginning with that letter.)

Sam, Sam, **do you love** Julie?
Yes, no, yes, no, yes, no . . .

Annie, Annie, **do you love** Ben?
Yes, no, yes, no, yes, no . . .

Names that are printed this way—Mary—are the
names of the jumpers and their friends.

IN AND OUT

Jumping in and out of the rope is fun—if you can do it gracefully. Many in-and-out rhymes let the jumper call in a friend by name.

——————————△ ▽ △——————————

Rooms for rent,
Inquire within.
As I move out
Let Rachel **come in.**

In, spin.
Let Laura **come in.**
Out, spout.
Let Laura **go out.**

I love coffee, I love tea,
I want Amy to come in with me.

Oh, in I run and around I go,
Clap my hands and nod just so.
I lift my knee and slap my shoe.
When I go out, let Ginny come in.

Callings in and callings out,
I call Rudy in.
Rudy's in and won't go out—
I call Kathie in.

Dancing Dolly had no sense.
She bought a fiddle for eighteen cents.
But the only tune that she could play
Was "Alex, get out of the donkey's way!"

(On the last line, "Alex" jumps out, and a new
jumper comes in.)

California oranges, fifty cents a pack.
Come on, Donna, and tap me on the back.

(At the end of the verse, "Donna" jumps in and
taps the jumper, who then jumps out.)

Gypsy, gypsy lived in a tent.
Gypsy, gypsy never paid rent.
She borrowed one,
She borrowed two,
And passed the rope over to YOU.

STREET GAMES

COIN BOWLING

You don't need bowling shoes for this game!

Number of players: Two or more
Object of game: To be the first to bowl the coin down

1. Balance a coin on its edge in the middle of a flat surface. Quarters, fifty-cent pieces, or silver dollars work best for this. If you have trouble balancing the coin, use a small spot of modeling clay to support it.

2. Players take turns rolling other coins across the surface, trying to knock over the balanced coin. It's harder than it looks, so players should aim at the flat side of the coin.

3. The first player to knock down the coin is the winner.

For a different game, set up several coins as in real bowling and award bonus points for knocking down more than one each time.

COIN TOSSING
Go ahead—throw your money away!

Number of players: Two or more
Object of game: To throw your coin closest to the wall

1. Using chalk, draw a line ten feet from a wall.

2. Give each player the same kind and same number of coins, anywhere from five to ten.

3. Players take turns standing behind the line and throwing a coin toward the wall.

4. The player whose coin is closest to the wall when all of the coins have been tossed is the winner.

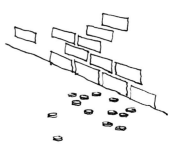

COVER IT
Send your coins running for cover!

Number of players: Two or more
Object of game: To cover the most coins

1. Using chalk, draw a line four feet from a wall.

2. Each player begins with five coins. Players take turns standing behind the line and tossing a coin against the wall.

3. If a player's coin is touching another coin when it comes to rest, he picks up both coins. If the coin isn't touching any others, he leaves it where it landed.

4. When a player runs out of coins, he is out of the game. Keep playing until one player has won all the coins.

You can play either of these games with anything flat and small enough to be thrown easily, such as playing cards or bottle caps. You can also move the line farther away from the wall or increase the number of pennies that each player starts with.

COIN CATCHING
Who can catch the most coins?

Number of players: Two or more
Object of game: To catch the most coins

1. Collect several of the same kind of coins; heavier ones like nickels and quarters work best.

2. The first player begins by balancing one coin on her elbow, as shown below:

3. She then drops her hand quickly, trying to catch the coin before it hits the ground.

4. Each player tries to do the same, and those who cannot do it on the first try are out.

5. When all the players have had their turn, a second coin is stacked on the first. The game continues with another round.

6. Play continues in this way, increasing the number of coins by one with each round, until one player is left. She is the winner!

HOPSCOTCH

Play all the variations of this ancient sidewalk game, then make up your own!

Number of players: Two to four

Object of game: To hop through the diagram and pick up your marker without making a mistake

1. Draw one of these diagrams on a sidewalk with a piece of chalk or scratch it into the dirt with a stick. Each square should be about eighteen inches on a side. Add a line several feet below the bottom of the diagram.

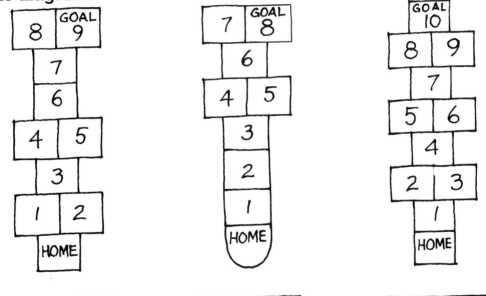

2. Each player will need a marker. You can use anything small and easy to throw. Coins, stones, keys, or bottle caps all work well.

3. The first player stands behind the line and throws her marker on square one.

4. Beginning at the Home square, the first player must hop on one foot through the squares in the diagram, skipping the first square. When two squares are side by side, the player should land with one foot in each square.

5. Once she hops to the square marked *Goal*, the player must turn around in one jump and then hop back through the diagram. When she reaches square two, she must lean down and pick up her marker, then hop into Home.

6. The first player continues her turn, throwing her marker into square two. She then hops through the diagram, this time skipping over square two (or any other square with a marker in it) both coming and going. She will have to stop on square three on her return trip to retrieve her marker from square two.

7. A player's turn continues upward through the squares unless she makes any of the following mistakes: stepping on a line, missing the target square with her marker or having her marker touch a line of the square, stepping on a square with anyone's marker in it, or putting two feet down in a single box.

8. When she makes a mistake, the player leaves her marker in the last square it occupied before her turn ended and waits for her turn to come around again. Then she must repeat the last round before she can throw her marker again.

9. If markers are blocking so many boxes that it becomes impossible to hop past them, temporary "boxies" can be drawn next to the occupied ones.

10. The first player to move her marker to the Goal and then hop back to Home is the winner.

RULE VARIATIONS

Instead of throwing her marker and then picking it up again, a player must kick her marker to the next square on her return trip. If she loses her balance or misses the target square, her turn is over.

When a player has gone through the entire diagram, she must hop to the Goal and back again, but this time she must balance the marker on one foot (or her head, finger, arm, knee, or forearm) while she is hopping.

CAT AND MOUSE

Mouse's fate is in your hands!

Number of players: Six or more
Object of game: To keep Cat away from Mouse!

1. Choose one player to be Mouse and another to be Cat. The rest of the players hold hands and form a circle, with Cat outside the circle and Mouse inside.

2. The game begins when Cat and Mouse say the following:
   Mouse: "I'm the mouse. You can't catch me!"
   Cat: "I'm the cat. We'll see! We'll see!"
Cat then tries to catch Mouse.

3. The other players try to help Mouse stay away from Cat. They drop hands to let Mouse pass and hold hands to keep Cat away.

4. When Mouse is caught, he joins the circle. Cat becomes Mouse for the next game, and a new player is picked to be Cat.

SIMON SAYS

Listen carefully to what Simon tells you to do!

Number of players: Three or more
Object of game: To be the last player left in the game

1. **Players stand in a group in front of the leader.**

2. **The leader gives a command and acts it out, such as "Simon says, Touch your toe" or "Turn around."**

3. **Players must follow the leader's command only when she begins by saying "Simon says..." If the leader doesn't say "Simon says," players must do nothing.**

4. **When a player follows a command that doesn't start with "Simon says," that player is out.**

5. **The last player left in the game becomes the new leader.**

RED LIGHT, GREEN LIGHT
Obey the stoplight and don't get caught!

Number of players: Four or more

Object of game: To be the first to reach the Stoplight without getting caught

1. One player is chosen to be the Stoplight, and the others line up at a starting line about thirty feet away.

2. The Stoplight has his back to the starting line and calls out "Green light!" Everyone begins to run toward him. In a moment, the Stoplight says "Red light!" and all the players must freeze and remain absolutely still.

3. After he calls "Red light," the Stoplight turns around quickly. If he sees any player moving, he sends that player back to the starting line to begin again.

4. The Stoplight continues to call out "Green light" then "Red light," trying to trick the other players by changing the timing between calls.

5. The first player to touch the Stoplight is the winner and becomes the Stoplight for the next game.

GIANT STEPS
Walk carefully and take big steps.

Number of players: Three or more
Object of game: To be the first to reach the leader

1. Players stand in a row against the wall at one end of the room.

2. The leader stands at the other end. He calls a player by name and gives a command. For example, "Mary, you may take three baby steps forward." The number and type of steps should vary with each player.

3. Mary must say, "May I?" If she does not, her turn is over, and she must go back to the wall.

4. If the leader says, "Yes, you may," Mary then takes three baby steps toward the leader.

5. If the leader says, "No, you may not," Mary must stay put.

6. The leader may also change the number or type of steps: "No, you may not. You may take two giant steps." Mary must remember to say, "May I?" again. If she does not, she must go all the way back to the wall and begin again.

7. The first player to reach the leader wins.

PAPER CRAFTS

JUMPING FROG
See how far you can make him hop!

You will need:

   1 square piece of paper, about 6 inches on each side

1. Fold the paper square in half horizontally, crease firmly, and then unfold.

2. Fold the square in half vertically, crease firmly, and then unfold.

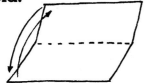

3. Fold each of the corners diagonally to the center.

4. Fold the top edges down to the middle line, creating a kite-shaped figure.

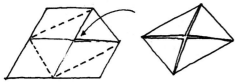

5. Fold the end of the kite, as shown.

6. Fold the bottom corners so that they meet on the middle line.

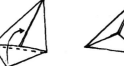

7. Fold the straight bottom up, and then fold half of it down again.

8. Fold the top triangle down to make his head and turn over your frog.

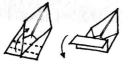

HOW TO MAKE HIM JUMP

Press lightly on the back of your frog and let your finger slide off. As you let go, he'll leap into the air!

SNAKE

A simple, scary, slithering serpent

You will need:

   1 square piece of thin paper

1. Fold the paper in half horizontally. Crease firmly, then unfold it. Fold the top and bottom edges to the center crease.

2. Fold each of the corners diagonally to meet at the center crease.

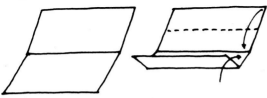

3. Fold the top and bottom edges again to meet in the center crease. Repeat this fold.

4. Fold your model in half along the center crease.

5. To make the neck, you will need to make a reverse fold about a third of the way down your model. Unfold one end partway and gently push the tip of the model upward so that the center crease reverses but only along the neck, as shown.

6. Unfold the very tip of the neck forward to form your snake's head.

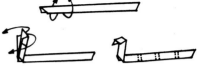

7. Make zigzag folds along the body of your snake to make it stand up on its own.

SAMURAI HELMET

Make this out of newspaper and wear it!

You will need:

    1 square piece of newspaper, about 18 inches on each side

1. Fold the paper square, as shown.

2. Fold each of the long corners down to meet at the point of the triangle.

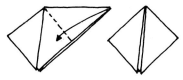

3. Fold these corners horizontally upward, leaving the bottom two layers of paper unfolded.

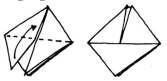

4. Fold these same corners outward to make the horns of your helmet.

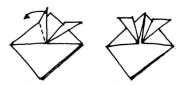

5. Lift the top layer of paper from the point of the triangle and fold it two-thirds of the way up toward the horns.

6. Fold the rest of this top layer upward along the center line.

7. Tuck the bottom layer inside your helmet—then open it up and put it on!

FORTUNE-TELLER
Predict the future for your friends!

You will need:

    1 square piece of paper

1. Fold each corner to the middle of the paper.

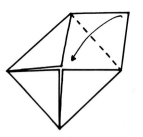

2. Turn the paper over and again fold the corners to the middle of the paper.

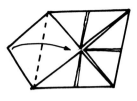

3. Turn the paper over again so that you are looking at four flaps of paper. Color each flap a different color or write the name of a different color on each flap.

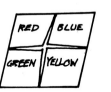

4. Turn over the Fortune-teller again and write a number on each of the eight triangles on the four flaps.

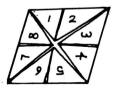

5. Lift each flap and write a fortune for each triangle.

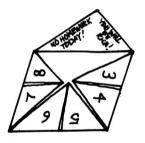

HOW TO USE YOUR FORTUNE-TELLER

1. Fold your Fortune-teller in half, as shown, and insert your fingers. The flaps with the colors should appear on top. Pinch your index finger and thumb together on each hand and pull to open your Fortune-teller one way. Press your two index fingers together and your thumbs together and push them apart to open your Fortune-teller the other way.

2. Ask a friend to pick a color. Spell the color out loud, opening your Fortune-teller in alternating directions with each letter (for the color yellow, you will open the Fortune-teller six times).

3. On the last letter, leave your fingers together so that the Fortune-teller is open. Ask your friend to pick one of the numbers shown. Count to that number, opening your Fortune-teller in alternating directions with each number.

4. On the last number, leave your Fortune-teller open and ask your friend to pick another number that is shown. Lift up the flap, and your friend's fortune will be revealed!

HELICOPTERS
Whirlybirds you can twirl anywhere

You will need:

> pencil
> tracing paper or thin white paper
> scissors
> thick paper
> staple or paper clip

1. Carefully copy the two helicopter shapes onto tracing paper and cut them out. Transfer the shapes onto thick paper by tracing around the thin paper pattern. Cut out your helicopters from the thick paper.

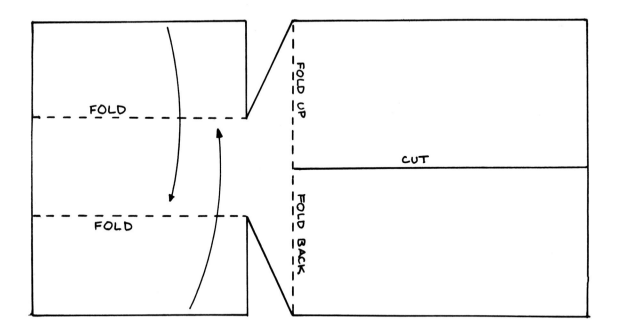

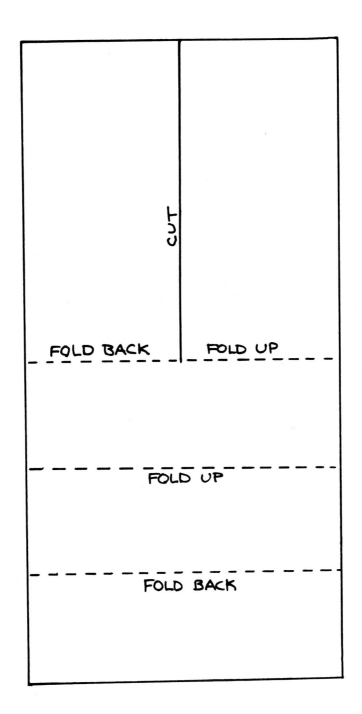

CUT

FOLD BACK | FOLD UP

FOLD UP

FOLD BACK

2. Fold along the dotted lines. For each helicopter, you will need to staple or clip the bottom flaps together. This will hold your helicopter together and give it the weight it needs to twirl properly.

3. Drop your helicopters from a high place and watch them twirl down.

DART GLIDER
This paper plane is built for speed.

You will need:

> 1 piece of paper, 8 1/2 x 11 inches
> paper clips

1. Fold the paper in half horizontally. Crease this fold and all others sharply with your thumb or finger.

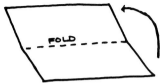

2. Fold down the top corners away from each other so that they meet along the center crease.

3. Fold down the tops, as shown, so that they meet along the center crease. Repeat this fold.

4. Release the top fold to form the wings. Paper clip the bottom of your plane to hold it together, and your dart glider is ready to fly!

AERIAL ACROBATICS

Your glider will fly a good distance with the wingtips flat. Try bending them up or down, as shown, to make your glider loop the loop or spin in midair. Challenge your friends to see who can make her glider perform the best stunts!

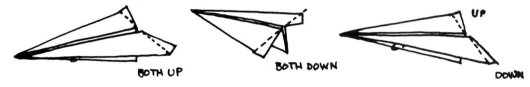

STUNT GLIDER
A loopy paper plane for midair stunts

You will need:

    1 piece of paper, 8 1/2 x 11 inches
    paper clips

1. Fold one corner of the paper diagonally, as shown.

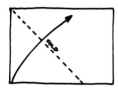

2. Fold the other corner across to form a point.

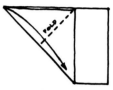

3. Fold about a half inch of the point back to form your glider's nose. Fold your glider in half, as shown, so the nose is inside the wings.

4. Fold down the wings, leaving about an inch for the body of your glider.

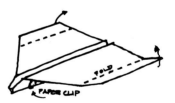

5. Fold up the wingtips and paper clip the body of your glider together. Ready for takeoff, Captain!

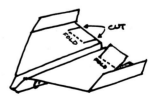

AERIAL ACROBATICS

This glider should make wide loops when you throw it. You can make it do extra loops and spins by cutting flaps into the wings, as shown, then bending the flaps up and down in different combinations. See which of your friends can make the loopiest plane!

POP-UP CARD
Liven up a handmade card with a surprise!

You will need:

    2 pieces of paper, 8 1/2 by 11 inches each
    scissors
    pens, pencils, markers, crayons, etc.
    glue

1. Fold both pieces of paper in half, but put one piece aside.

2. Cut two straight lines about 1 inch apart into the folded edge of the paper, as shown.

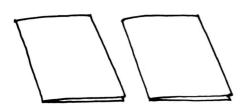

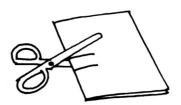

3. Fold the flap and make a crease, then unfold it.

4. Unfold the paper and press the strip, as shown, until it pops through to the other side. Turn over the paper and refold it in the middle. Make sure that the pop-up strip remains on the inside of your card.

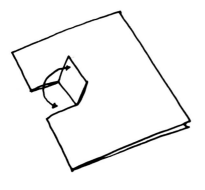

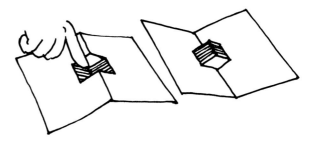

5. Draw and cut out a small figure to attach to the pop-up strip and glue it to the bottom half of the flap on the inside.

6. Glue the other piece of paper to the back of the paper with your pop-up strip. Be careful not to put glue on the strip itself.

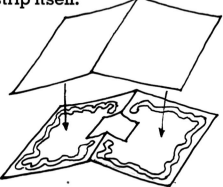

7. Now add drawings and words to the inside and outside of your card to complete it.

POP-UP VARIATIONS

Try these cuts for different pop-up shapes:

House

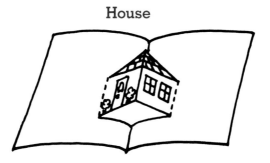

Egg

Butterfly

TRIANGLE POP-UP
A bigger pop-up for a bigger surprise!

You will need:

    2 pieces of paper, 8 1/2 by 11 inches each

    glue

    pens, pencils, markers, crayons, etc.

    scissors

1. Fold both pieces of paper in half.

2. Take one piece and fold one corner of the already folded side into a triangle.

3. Unfold the paper and pull the triangle outward, as shown. Refold the paper so that the triangle is no longer visible.

4. Glue the other piece of paper to the back of the paper with your pop-up triangle. Be careful not to put glue on the triangle pop-up itself.

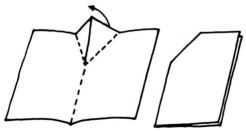

5. Draw and cut out a figure that you would like to appear on this pop-up.

6. Fold your figure vertically and put glue on the back of it. Attach it to your triangle pop-up, lining up the fold on your figure with the fold on the pop-up.

7. Draw decorations and write words on your card.

ARTS AND CRAFTS

WEAVING

A simple way to make hundreds of craft projects!

You will need:

> rectangle of thick cardboard, 9 by 12 inches
> scissors
> safety pin
> strips of cloth, 1/4 to 1/2 inch thick

1. Cut notches 1/4 inch apart into the 9-inch sides of the cardboard. Tie a strip of cloth to one corner of the cardboard, then wrap it back and forth between the notches, as shown below. Tie the other end of the strip at the corner of the rectangle that is diagonally across from the one you began with. You have now made your loom.

2. Attach another strip of cloth to the safety pin and close the pin. Begin weaving by threading the pin under the first strip at the top of your loom. Push the pin over the next strip, then under the one after it. Continue in this way, over and under, all the way across the loom.

3. When you reach the end of your loom, weave back the way you came, looping the cloth strips, as shown. This time, however, go under each strip you went over the first time, and over each strip you went under.

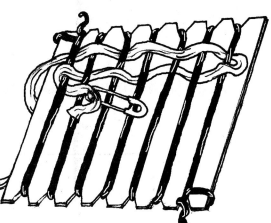

4. Continue this for each row you want to weave, pulling the cloth strip over and under the loom. Make sure not to pull the strip too tight, or the edges of your final product will not be even.

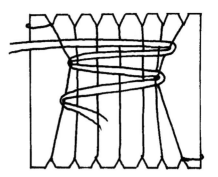

WRONG

5. Once you have woven a few rows, push the rows snugly together. If you come to the end of a strip of your weaving material and want to keep weaving, tie on a new strip with a strong double knot.

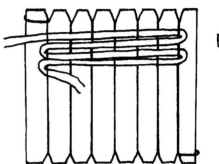

RIGHT

6. When you have finished weaving, be sure you are at the end of a row. Tie off each end of your cloth to the loom strip next to it and lift both strip ends off the loom. To remove your work from the loom, bend down the tabs between the notches and slide the loom out. You can also break the loom by cutting it in half and removing the pieces.

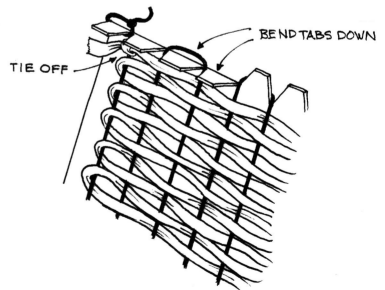

TIE OFF

BEND TABS DOWN

WEAVING PROJECT SUGGESTIONS

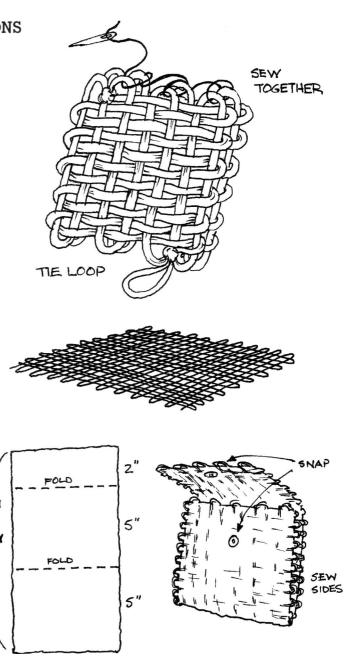

Pot Holder

Weave two squares of the same size out of candle wicking (available at a crafts store). Sew the two squares together and tie a loop to one corner of your pot holder so that it can be hung up.

SEW TOGETHER

TIE LOOP

Place Mat

Make the notches on your loom 1/8 inch apart so that the weave will be finer. Use soft cotton string for both the loom and your weaving material.

Pocketbook

Use thick cloth strips in a rectangular loom. When you have finished weaving, fold the rectangle, as shown, and sew the sides of the pocketbook up. Add a snap so that your pocketbook will stay closed.

FOLD   2"

FOLD   5"

5"

SNAP

SEW SIDES

Think up some projects of your own! You can use different size looms as long as the sides of the loom measure to whole inches and not fractions.

PLAY DOUGH

Even Michelangelo had to start somewhere.

You will need:
>bowl
>2 cups flour
>1 cup salt
>2 tablespoons cooking oil
>3/4 cup water
>food coloring

1. Mix the flour and salt together in a bowl.

2. Add the oil and a few drops of the food coloring to the water.

3. Pour the water mixture slowly into the flour mixture, kneading with your hands until it becomes soft and doughy.

4. Make projects for your family and friends.

5. You can dry your projects in a 250° F oven for 1 1/2 to 2 hours or let them air-dry. When the play dough is dry, decorate with poster or acrylic paints.

NOTE: This play dough should <u>not</u> be eaten.

DO NOT EAT!

PLAY DOUGH YOU CAN EAT
Make delicious sculptures and eat them!

You will need:
- bowl
- 2 cups powdered dry milk
- 2 cups smooth peanut butter
- 1 cup honey

1. Mix the ingredients together in a bowl and stir until well blended.

2. Make projects for your family and friends or create interesting edible party favors.

3. Projects can be decorated with raisins, shredded coconut, or other treats. These projects cannot be saved. They are made to be eaten!

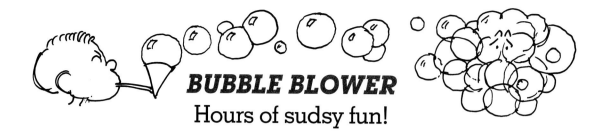

BUBBLE BLOWER
Hours of sudsy fun!

You will need:

To make bubbles:
1/4 cup liquid dish detergent
1 tablespoon vegetable oil
1 quart warm water

To make a pipe:
paper milk carton
scissors
pencil
drinking glass
tape
straw

BUBBLES
Mix liquid dish detergent and vegetable oil in warm water.

PIPE
1. Clean out a used paper milk carton, cut out one side, and lay the side flat, as shown in step 2.

2. Trace the top of the glass onto the milk carton panel, cut out the circle, and then cut the circle in half.

3. Roll the half circle together to form a cone, then tape the edges of the cone together. Poke a small hole in the bottom of the cone.

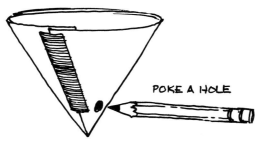

POKE A HOLE

4. Insert the straw into the hole. Then spoon the bubble mix into your pipe and blow lots of bubbles!

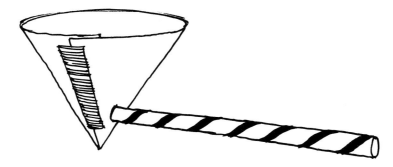

If you have trouble getting your pipe to make bubbles, hold it upside down when you blow.

MOTORBOAT
A tub-time toy that doesn't need batteries

You will need:

> waxed cardboard
> scissors
> pencil
> ruler
> waterproof tape (such as duct tape or strong packing tape)
> Ivory bar soap

1. To make your boat, you will need to find some waxed cardboard, like the kind used for milk and ice-cream cartons or boxes of butter. Wash out the carton well.

2. Cut a 2 inch by 3 inch rectangle out of one side of your carton. Find the center of a short side of the rectangle, then use a ruler to mark a straight line from this center point to the corners at the opposite end. Fold up along these lines.

3. Tape up the end of the boat with the waterproof tape. Add the motor below to get your boat moving!

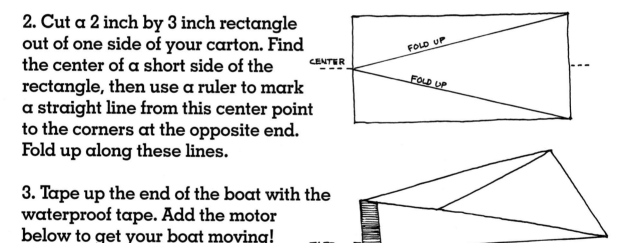

4. Cut a very small wedge from the soap. Then cut a hole from the back of your boat, making it smaller than the wedge.

5. Put your boat in a half-full sink, bathtub, or other quiet water. Place the soap wedge into the hole in your boat so that the point of the wedge is touching the water. The rest of the wedge sits on top of the boat. Now watch your boat move forward!

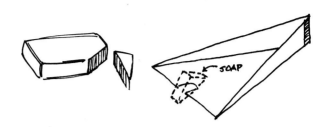

BOOMERANG

A curvy toy that comes back to you every time

You will need:

        tracing paper or thin white paper
        pencil
        scissors
        stiff cardboard
        2 books

1. Carefully copy the boomerang shape shown here onto tracing paper and cut it out. Transfer the shape onto the cardboard by tracing around this thin paper pattern. Cut out your boomerang from the cardboard.

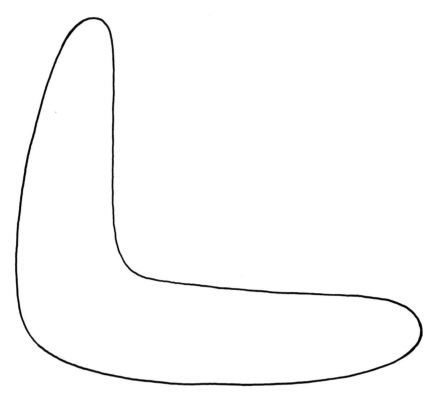

2. To launch your boomerang, put it on the back of your hand with the long end hanging over the edge. Snap it sharply with your index finger, and it should curve away from you and then return.

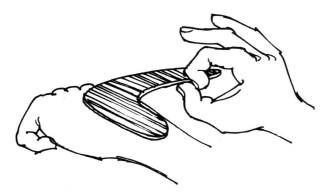

3. If you have trouble with this method, create a launching pad with two books. Put your boomerang on one of the books with the long end hanging over the edge. Lift up the end of the book opposite to the boomerang and put the second book underneath this end. The book on top should form a ramp that slopes gently toward the boomerang. Snap the boomerang off the book by flicking its tip with the eraser end of a pencil.

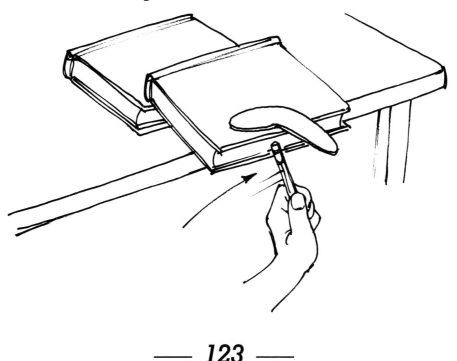

POTATO PRINTING

Make your own homemade stamp.

You will need:
> several small dishes
> paper towels
> ink, tempera paint, or food coloring
> potato
> knife
> paper

1. First, you will need to make the ink pads for your stamp. Line the bottoms of several small dishes with a few layers of paper towels, trimming the parts of the towels that hang over the edge.

2. Soak the towels with ink, tempera paint, or food coloring, using a different dish for each color you want to use.

3. To make your stamps, cut a potato in half and carve a design into the flat end of the potato. You will need to cut away the parts you don't want to print, and you will need to carve letters backward.

NOTE: Use a knife <u>only</u> with adult supervision or permission.

4. Press your design into one of the colored inks and stamp the potato onto gift wrap, stationery, book jackets, greeting cards, shelf paper, or anything that you think deserves your special stamp.

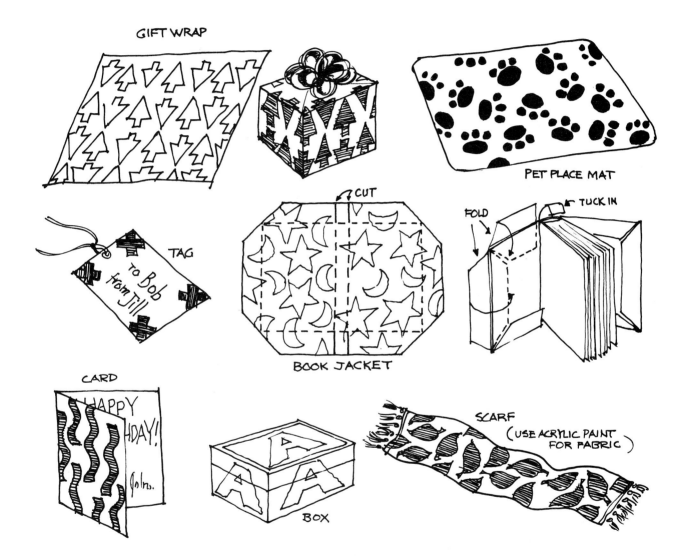

GIFT WRAP

PET PLACE MAT

TAG

To Bob from Jill

CUT

BOOK JACKET

FOLD

TUCK IN

CARD

HAPPY HDAY!

John.

BOX

SCARF
(USE ACRYLIC PAINT FOR FABRIC)

ETCHINGS

Create beautiful multicolored pictures.

You will need:

    crayons, including black
    stiff white paper
    black ink
    paintbrush
    nail or nail file

1. Use light-colored crayons to fill a stiff piece of white paper with patches and stripes. Push down hard so that the colors go on thickly.

2. Cover the patches and stripes with black crayon or brush over them with two coats of black ink, allowing the ink to dry between coats. Make sure the colors are completely covered.

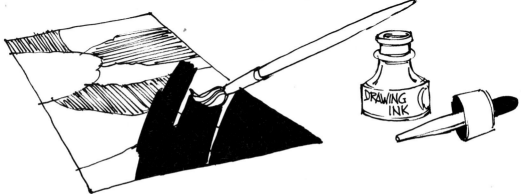

3. With a nail, nail file, or another pointed tool, scratch a picture on the black surface. As you gently scrape away the black layer, the light colors of your first crayon layer will come peeking through.

Use this etching technique to make beautiful artwork for friends and family.

WORD GAMES

TELEPHONE
Have you heard the latest gossip?

Number of players: Five or more
Object of game: To try to keep the story straight

1. Players sit in a circle or a line. The more players you have, the sillier the game gets.

2. Choose one player to begin. That player makes up a short sentence and whispers it to the player to his left.

3. This player repeats what she heard, or what she thinks she heard, into the ear of the person to her left. Each player must listen carefully, because the sentence cannot be repeated.

4. The sentence continues around the circle until it reaches the player on the other side of the first player. She says the sentence she heard, and then the first player says what the original sentence was. The differences are often hilarious!

TWENTY QUESTIONS
Which one of your friends is the best detective?

Number of players: Three or more
Object of game: To figure out the mystery word

1. Choose one player to be the leader. She must have in mind the name of an object or famous person for the other players to guess.

2. The other players take turns asking questions about the mystery word or name that can be answered "Yes" or "No." Good questions will build on the answers to previous questions. If players find out that the leader has chosen a person's name, they might try to determine if that person is alive or dead, a man or a woman, and what the person is famous for.

3. The first person to guess the mystery word correctly on or before the twentieth question is the leader for the next game. If no one can guess the mystery by the twentieth question, the leader chooses another mystery word, and the game begins again.

Twenty Questions usually begins with the question "Is it animal, vegetable, or mineral?" This is the only question allowed that cannot be answered "Yes" or "No." The mystery word is considered "animal" if it is a person or animal or if it comes from an animal. A lion, a doctor, and a leather briefcase are all "animal." The word is "vegetable" if it is some kind of plant or comes from a plant. A flower, a carrot, and a cotton shirt are all "vegetable." Everything else is "mineral." This includes anything made of stone, metal, or plastic. This first question will help players narrow down the possibilities and make the game a little easier to win.

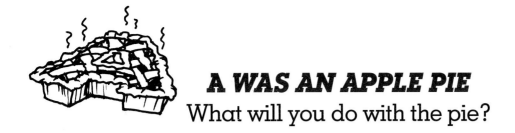

A WAS AN APPLE PIE
What will you do with the pie?

Number of players: Three or more
Object of game: To make up sentences for each letter of the alphabet

1. The first player begins by saying, "A was an apple pie, and A ate it."

2. The second player then continues, using the letter B in the same way: "B baked it" or "B bit it."

3. The next player makes up a sentence beginning with C, such as "C cut it." And so on through the alphabet.

4. Players should give their answers quickly, so that a player who hesitates for too long is out. The last player in is the winner.

Another option is to have players think of an action word and a descriptive word beginning with the proper letters. For example: "A ate it angrily," "B baked it badly," and so forth. You can also make up other phrases to begin with, such as "A was an automobile" or "A was Alan."

BUZZ
Think counting's easy? Try it this way!

Number of players: Two or more
Object of game: To count using "buzz" in place of certain numbers

1. Players should sit in a circle. The first player begins counting with "One."

2. The second player says "Two," and so forth, counting upward with each player. But every time a player reaches a number that has a seven in it (seven, seventeen, twenty-seven, thirty-seven, etc.) or is a multiple of seven (seven, fourteen, twenty-one, twenty-eight, thirty-five, etc.), he must say "Buzz" instead of that number.

3. The game should move along quickly, and any player who says a number when he should have said "Buzz" or says "Buzz" in the wrong place is out of the circle.

4. Counting continues with the number that was said incorrectly. The last player left is the winner!

FIZZ-BUZZ

For a variation, play Fizz-Buzz. This is just like Buzz, except that players say "Fizz" when they reach five and its multiples, while still saying "Buzz" at the proper times. So one through twenty would be: "One, two, three, four, fizz, six, buzz, eight, nine, fizz, eleven, twelve, thirteen, buzz, fizz, sixteen, buzz, eighteen, nineteen, fizz."

To make the game even more challenging, try using "Buzz" for three and "Fizz" for four and specify the factors. For example: "One, two, buzz, fizz, five, buzz times two, seven, fizz times two, buzz times buzz."

BOOO! UH, BHOOO-
NO, BUHH, UH...

GHOST
This game's only scary if you can't spell.

Number of players: Best with two to four
Object of game: To avoid spelling out a word

1. The game begins when one player says a letter out loud. The next player adds a letter to this one, thinking of a word that begins with these two letters.

2. In turn, each person adds a letter to the end of the chain, as long as the new letter can still begin a longer word but does not yet complete a "legal" word. A legal word is any word that is found in a dictionary, or any name of a person or a place. When each player has given a letter, the game continues with the first player.

3. If a player adds a letter to the chain that doesn't sound like it could form part of a word, another player may challenge her letter. If she cannot name a word beginning with the letter chain that includes her letter, she is a ghost and out of the game. For example, if the first three letters are *B-U-L-*, and the next player says *"X,"* another player may challenge the person who said *"X."* That player must then name a word beginning with *B-U-L-X-* (an impossible task, because there is no such word).

4. If the letter he says completes a word, that player is a ghost and out of the game. This is true even if the player finishes a shorter word in the process of spelling out a longer one. For example, if a player adds an *N* to *W-I-*, wanting to spell *WINDOW*, he has nonetheless finished the word *WIN* and is a ghost.

5. Once one player becomes a ghost, the letter chain begins again with the person following the ghost. Keep playing until one player is left. She is the winner!

For a longer game, try this variation. When a player makes her first mistake, she is not immediately out of the game. Instead of being a *GHOST*, she is just a *G*. After her second mistake, she is a *GH*, and a *GHO* after her third mistake. This continues until she is a *GHOST* and is out of the game.

GEOGRAPHY
The fastest way to get from Japan to Nevada

Number of players: Two or more
Object of game: To use the last letter of a word as the first letter of a new word

1. The first player begins the game by giving the name of a geographical location, either a city, state, country, body of water, mountain, or island. Players can decide at the beginning of the game whether to allow all of these categories or only certain ones, for example, just the names of cities.

2. The next player must say another place whose name begins with the *last* letter of the word given by the first player. For example, if the first player says "Mississippi," then the second player could say "Indiana," the third player could say "Arkansas," and so on.

3. If a player repeats another player's word, or cannot give a word within a fair amount of time, she is out. The game continues with the next player. The last player to remain in is the winner!

Geography can be played with other categories, too, such as the names of famous people or fictional characters, movie or book titles, or whatever else you and your friends find interesting.

TABOO
Whatever you do, don't say it!

Number of players: Three or more
Object of game: To answer questions without using certain letters of the alphabet

1. The first player tells everyone a letter of the alphabet that will be forbidden, or "taboo." She then asks the other players any question she likes.

2. Players take turns answering her question, using sensible phrases or sentences that do not contain the forbidden letter. The game should move quickly, with each player given only five seconds to come up with an answer.

3. If a player uses the taboo letter or gives an answer that doesn't make sense or doesn't answer the question, he is out.

4. When all players have had a turn, the first player asks a new question, keeping the same taboo letter. Play continues among the remaining players.

5. The last player remaining is the winner and chooses a new taboo letter and question for the next game.

HINK PINKS

This name game is a fun one.

Number of players: Three or more
Object of game: To make up or guess paired rhyming phrases

1. One player thinks of a hink pink. A hink pink is made up of two one-syllable words that rhyme. For example, a pile of between-meal goodies is a "snack stack." Once the player has thought of a hink pink, she tells its definition to the other players. For example, thinking of a "mouse house," the first player tells the others, "A rodent's dwelling."

2. The other players take turns trying to guess what the hink pink is.

3. The first person to figure out the hink pink gets to make up her own, and the other players must guess what her hink pink is.

When you've run out of hink pinks, it's time to move on to "hinkie pinkies." A hinkie pinkie is like a hink pink, except it's made up of two two-syllable words. Here are some hinkie pinkies to get you started:

A tow-truck inspector—"wrecker checker"
A daisy's strength—"flower power"
A New York ball player who just struck out—"cranky Yankee"
A bigger battery—"larger charger"

INITIAL LETTERS
All you have to know is your name.

Number of players: Three or more
Object of game: To answer questions with words that begin with your first initial

1. **Players sit in a circle. The first player begins by asking a question that is as simple or as silly as he likes.**

2. **Each player answers the question, in turn, with one word that begins with the initial letter of his or her first name. For example, if the question is "What is your favorite color?" Peter could answer "Purple."**

3. **The game should move quickly, with each player given only five seconds to come up with an answer. If a player is not able to come up with an answer in this time, or gives an answer that doesn't match his or her initial, that player is out.**

4. **The round ends when it is the first player's turn to answer. The second player then asks a new question, and the game continues among the remaining players. The last player to stay in is the winner!**

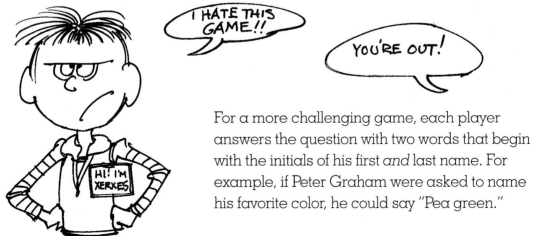

I HATE THIS GAME!!

YOU'RE OUT!

For a more challenging game, each player answers the question with two words that begin with the initials of his first *and* last name. For example, if Peter Graham were asked to name his favorite color, he could say "Pea green."

ANAGRAMS
Scrambled letters to scramble your brain

Number of players: One or more
Object of game: To make up word pairs that have the same letters

1. Get paper and a pencil and try making up some anagrams. An anagram is a word or phrase with the same letters as another word or phrase but in a different order. For example, *stack* and *tacks* are anagrams because they are both made up of the letters *A, C, K, S,* and *T.* Anagrams are the most fun when the words or phrases are related:

The eyes. They see.   The countryside. No city dust here.

2. Once you have three or more anagrams, make two columns on a piece of paper. Write the original words in one column. Write their anagram pairs in the second column in a different order.

3. Challenge your friends to match up each word with its anagram pair.

Here's a sample game board:

Word	Anagram
HORSE	RACES
SMILE	ALLOY
LOYAL	MILES
SCARE	SHORE
STOVE	VOTES

PALINDROMES
A truly backward game—or is it?

Number of players: One or more

Object of game: To make up phrases that are the same forward or backward

A palindrome is a word or phrase that is spelled the same forward and backward, not counting punctuation or spaces between letters. Some examples:

Mom	Llama mall
Dad	Evil Olive
Wow	No lemon, no melon.
Anna	Drowsy sword
Madam, I'm Adam.	A man, a plan, a canal, Panama

Spend some time thinking up some palindromes of your own. (Paper and a pencil might be helpful.) Get together with your friends and see who can come up with the best ones!

BRAINTEASERS

COLOR BY NUMBERS

This secret code is tough—you can count on it.

Each of the following words is a color, written in a code that substitutes numbers for letters. The same code is used for all five colors. Can you figure out what colors are spelled out here? Answers on page 190.

a. 25-5-12-12-15-23
b. 7-18-5-5-14
c. 18-5-4
d. 15-18-1-14-7-6
e. 2-18-15-23-14

<u>Y</u> <u>E</u> <u>L</u> <u>L</u> <u>O</u> <u>W</u>

The first answer is given. Now you know which letters the first five numbers stand for. Use these to help figure out the rest. For more fun, think up your own code and send secret messages to your friends.

GOTCHA!
Sneaky math problems

Don't work too fast on these puzzles, because the answer's not always what it seems to be. Answers on page 190.

1. How much does a brick weigh if it weighs five pounds plus half its own weight?

2. How much is twice half of 987,654,321?

3. Divide 20 by 1/2 and add 3. What is the result?

4. A farmer had seventeen sheep. All but nine died. How many were left?

5. How much is 1 times 2 times 3 times 4 times 5 times 6 times 7 times 8 times 9 times 0?

TEST YOUR MEMORY
How much can your brain hold?

Study the picture below for as long as you like. Try to remember as many details as you can. When you think you've seen everything, turn to page 190 and answer the questions about this picture.

LOGIC TIME
Twist your brain around these puzzlers.

RAFFLE BAFFLE

All four of these children won prizes at the school raffle, but then they got their tickets and prizes all mixed up. Match up each person with his or her raffle ticket and the prize each ticket won. Answers on page 190.

JANET AND DOUG HAVE LIGHT HAIR. I WON AN AIR RIFLE.

I DIDN'T WIN THE TEDDY BEAR. ALAN DID.

MY RAFFLE TICKET NUMBER STARTS WITH A 6.

MY NUMBER DIVIDES BY 4 JUST LIKE DOREEN'S. I DIDN'T WIN THE HOUSEPLANT.

A — 2484

B — 1974

C — 4308 — NOT DOREEN'S TICKET

D — 6423 — WON THE CANDY

DOG SHOW

These dogs were separated from their masters. Can you figure out which dog belongs with which owner and the names of each pair? Answers on page 190.

LOONY LINES AND PAPER PROBLEMS
A grab bag of brainteasers

Try to draw each of the figures below without crossing or redrawing a line and without lifting your pencil from the paper. Answers on page 191.

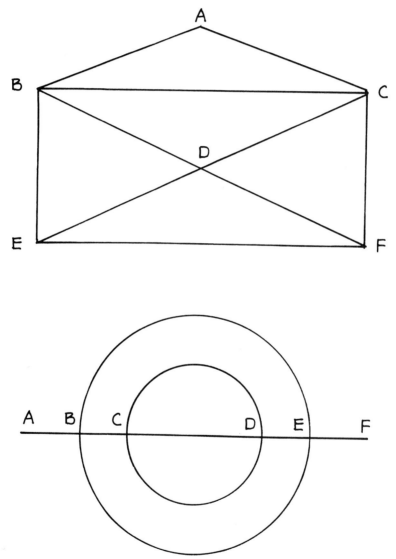

Draw each of the two figures below onto separate sheets of heavy paper or cardboard, then cut them into pieces along the solid lines. Rearrange the pieces of figure A to form a rectangle and those of figure B to form a square. Answers on page 191.

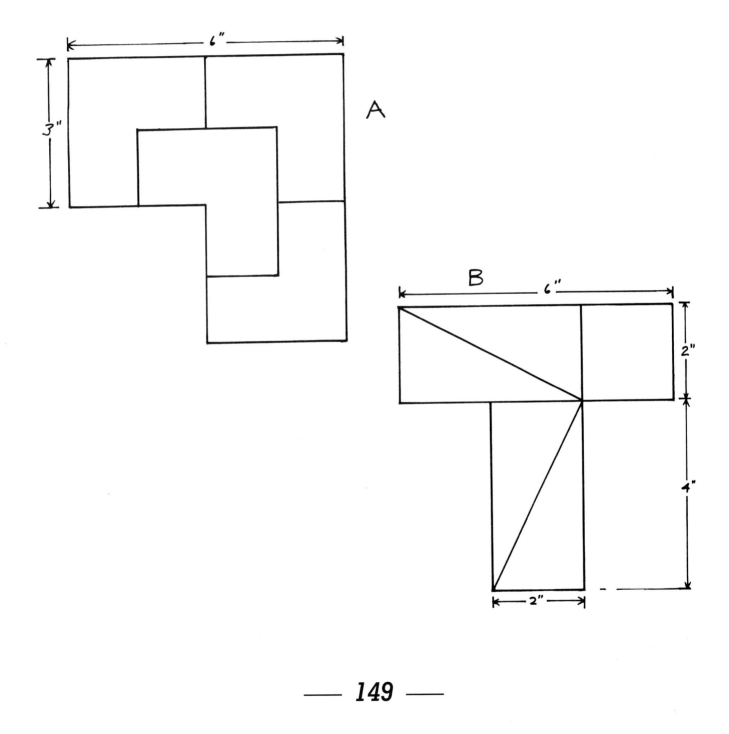

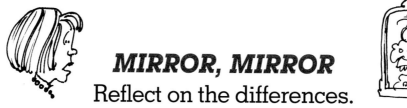

MIRROR, MIRROR
Reflect on the differences.

Doug drew this beautiful picture of a house by a lake. But he made some mistakes when he drew the reflection in the lake—eleven mistakes, to be exact. Can you find them? Answer on page 191.

ROLL OVER, ROVER
A dog-gone difficult dilemma

Get thirteen matches or toothpicks and arrange them to make the dog shown here. As you can see, he's facing to the left now. By moving only two matches, can you make him face the other way? Answer on page 191.

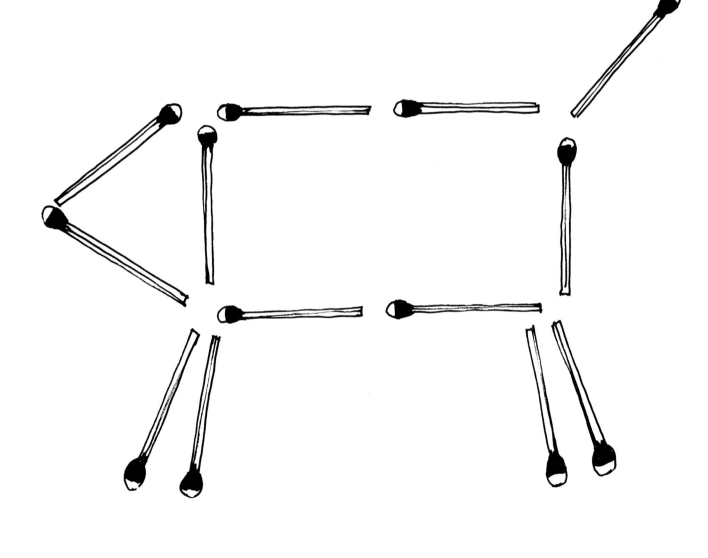

TWO PERFECT SQUARES
There's no match for this puzzle.

Arrange twelve matches (or toothpicks) into the diagram shown here, which forms four squares. By removing only two matches, can you reduce the number of squares to just two? Answer on page 191.

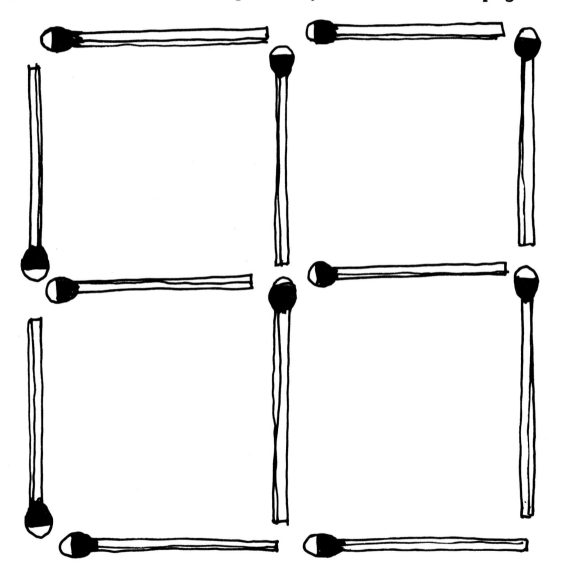

THE LAST OF THE BRAINTEASERS
Two final stumpers

1. If you only have a five-quart bottle and a three-quart bottle and have to measure out exactly seven quarts, how would you do it?

2. A hen can lay an egg and a half in a day and a half. How many days would it take twenty-five of these hens to lay twenty-five eggs?

Answers on page 192.

PAPER AND PENCIL GAMES

UP THE LADDER
Keep climbing!

Number of Players: Two
Object of game: To be first to mark your way to the top of the ladder

1. On a piece of paper, draw a ladder with seven or more rungs. Write *Finish* above the top rung.

2. Players take turns making three marks in the empty spaces between the rungs of the ladder. The first player's mark is an *X*, and the second player uses an *O*.

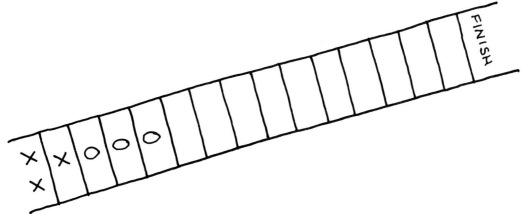

3. Each player can divide his marks up any way he wants, putting all three in one space, putting one each in three different spaces, or some other combination.

4. Neither player can put his mark in a space already occupied by other marks, and skipping rungs is not allowed.

5. The first player to put his mark in the *Finish* space wins.

Change the number of rungs and play again for a completely different game!

HANGMAN

Guess the mystery word or be hanged!

Number of players: Two or more
Object of game: To guess the mystery word before you get hanged

1. Choose one player to be the Hangman. The Hangman then thinks up a mystery word for the other players to guess.

2. On a blank sheet of paper, the Hangman writes one dash for each letter of the mystery word. For example, the word *garbage* **would have seven dashes.**

3. The other players take turns guessing letters in the mystery word. If the letter is in the word, the Hangman writes it above the appropriate dash or dashes.

4. If the guess is wrong, the Hangman draws the base of the gallows. For each wrong guess that follows, the Hangman adds another part to the gallows. Once the gallows is finished, each wrong guess adds one body part hanging from the gallows, beginning with the head. The complete figure looks like this.

5. Players should keep track of their wrong guesses by writing those letters next to the gallows.

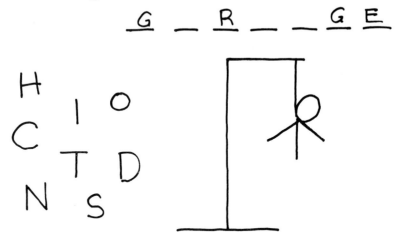

G _ R _ _ G E

H
I   O
C
T   D
N   S

6. If a player guesses the word before the Hangman finishes drawing a body on the gallows, that player wins!

G A R B A G E

For a more difficult game, choose a mystery phrase or well-known saying. You can also make the game last longer by drawing more body parts—a face, hands, or feet.

JOTTO
Use the clues to figure out the Mastermind's mystery word.

Number of players: Two
Object of game: To guess the mystery word

1. One player, called the Mastermind, secretly writes a word at the top of a piece of lined paper, then folds the paper just enough to hide her word from the other player.

2. Below the fold, the Mastermind then draws two columns, one called Guesses and the other called Score. In the first line of the Guesses column, the Mastermind writes one dash for each letter in her mystery word.

3. The other player begins by guessing any word with the same number of letters as the mystery word. He writes his guess in the first line of the Guesses column. The Mastermind then compares his guess with her hidden word.

4. For every letter in his guess that is the same as a letter in her mystery word and is in the same location, the Mastermind writes a + in the Score column. For example, if her mystery word is *FARM* and his guess is *CAKE*, the Mastermind would write one +, because *A* is the second letter of both *CAKE* and *FARM*.

5. For every letter in his guess that is the same as one in her mystery word but is in a different location, the Mastermind writes a - in the Score column. For the mystery word *FARM*, a guess of *CROW* would score a -, because the *R* is correct but is the second letter of his guessed word and the third letter of her mystery word.

6. The Mastermind does not write anything for letters in his guessed word that are not in her mystery word, so sometimes the Score column will be blank.

7. The other player then guesses a word based on the previous words and writes his new guess in the next line of the Guesses column. For each + in the Score column, he should keep one letter in the same place as the first word, and he should keep one letter for each - but move it to a new position in the new word. If the Score column is blank, he should guess a word with all new letters.

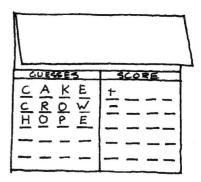

8. The Mastermind then scores his new guess in the next line of the Score column. Sometimes a guess with a correct letter or two may be followed by a new guess with no score at all!

9. Guessing continues until the other player figures out the Mastermind's mystery word. The other player then becomes the Mastermind.

TIC-TAC-TOE

A classic pencil game, with some new twists

Number of players: Two
Object of game: To get three marks in a row

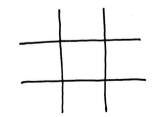

1. To play regular tic-tac-toe, draw the game board on a blank piece of paper.

2. The first player writes an *X* in one of the game spaces, and the second player follows by writing an *O* in another space.

3. The two players take turns making their marks, and the first one to get three in a row (up, down, or from corner to corner) is the winner. In case of a tie, in which neither player gets three in a row, play again.

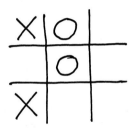

TIC-TAC-TOE SQUARED

1. Draw the same game board as in Tic-Tac-Toe, but draw a square around the whole board to make nine boxes.

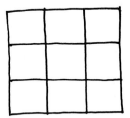

2. Players take turns as in Tic-Tac-Toe, but they make their marks where the lines cross, rather than in the spaces in between the lines. The outside lines are included in the game board so that there are sixteen places to make a mark.

3. Even though it is possible to make four marks in a row, the winner is still the first player to get three consecutive marks.

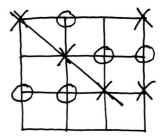

TIC-TAC-TOE-TOE

1. Add another row and column of boxes to the Tic-Tac-Toe Squared board so that there are sixteen boxes in all.

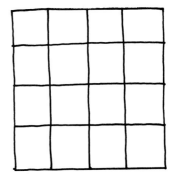

2. As in Tic-Tac-Toe Squared, the players make their marks at the intersections of lines and not in the spaces in between the lines.

3. To win Tic-Tac-Toe-Toe, however, a player must get *four* consecutive marks, although it is possible to make five marks in a row on the game board.

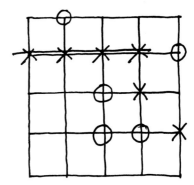

For a longer, more challenging game, make an even bigger board and try to get five marks in a row!

SQUIGGLES
Make it pretty or silly!

Number of players: Two or more
Object of game: To take turns drawing a picture

1. The first player draws a squiggly line on a blank piece of paper.

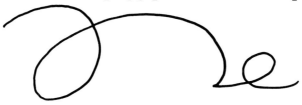

2. The next player must draw a picture, using this line as some part of the drawing.

3. When the player finishes her picture, she makes a squiggle on a new piece of paper and passes it along to the next player, who turns the new squiggle into another picture.

Be as creative as possible! You can even combine several squiggle drawings together to make a scene.

DOTS

Connect the dots to make the most squares and win!

Number of players: Two or more
Object of game: To claim the most squares

1. To make the playing board, draw a grid with an equal number of rows and columns of dots. Ten rows and ten columns is a good size to start.

2. Each player takes turns drawing a line between two dots that are next to each other. The lines may go in any direction except diagonally.

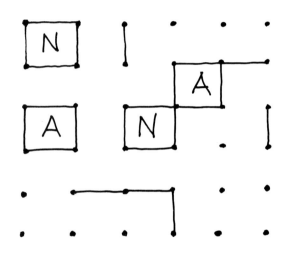

3. Whenever a player draws a line that completes a square, she writes her first initial in the middle of the square and takes another turn.

4. If she is able to, the player can use this extra turn to complete another square. With proper planning, a player can make lots of squares in a row, especially late in the game.

5. When the board is filled, players count up the number of squares they made. The one with the most squares wins!

TRIANGLES
Try this new angle on Dots.

Number of players: Two or more
Object of game: To claim the most triangles

1. On a blank piece of paper, make rows of dots to form a triangle. The first row will have only one dot, the second will have two dots, the third will have three, and so forth. Make the game board as big or small as you like.

2. Players take turns connecting two dots with a line, either horizontally or diagonally.

3. Whenever a player draws a line that completes a triangle, she puts her first initial in the triangle and takes another turn. As in Dots, one player can continue to make triangles with each free turn.

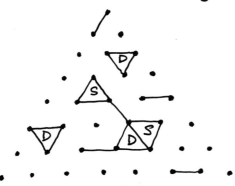

4. When the game board is filled, count up the triangles made by each player. The one with the most triangles wins.

For a more difficult game, award extra points for making larger triangles. Keep track of these bonus points at the same time they are earned, because it will be too complicated to count these bigger triangles at the end of the game.

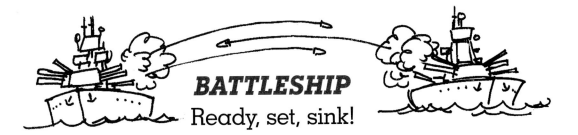

BATTLESHIP
Ready, set, sink!

Number of players: Two
Object of game: To be first to sink your opponent's ships

1. Each player draws two separate grids of ten rows and ten columns on a blank piece of paper. That way each player has two large squares, each containing one hundred smaller squares. Graph paper is best for this game.

2. Mark the rows on each grid with the numbers one through ten and the columns with the letters *A* through *J*. Each player marks the left grid *Ships* and the right grid *Shots*.

3. Without letting his opponent see, each player places five "ships," either horizontally or vertically, on the Ships grid. This is done by shading the correct number of squares in a row for each ship and writing the name of the ship near the squares it occupies. Each player has an aircraft carrier (which fills five spaces), a battleship (five spaces), a cruiser (four spaces), a destroyer (three spaces), and a submarine (two spaces).

4. When both players have placed all their ships, the first player begins by calling out a square where he thinks his opponent's ships might be. Grid squares are named with the letter and number that correspond to the column and row the square occupies (A-8, C-10, or F-1, for example).

5. If the player calls out a square on which one of his opponent's ships is located, the second player says "Hit!" and tells him which ship he has hit. Otherwise, the second player says "Miss."

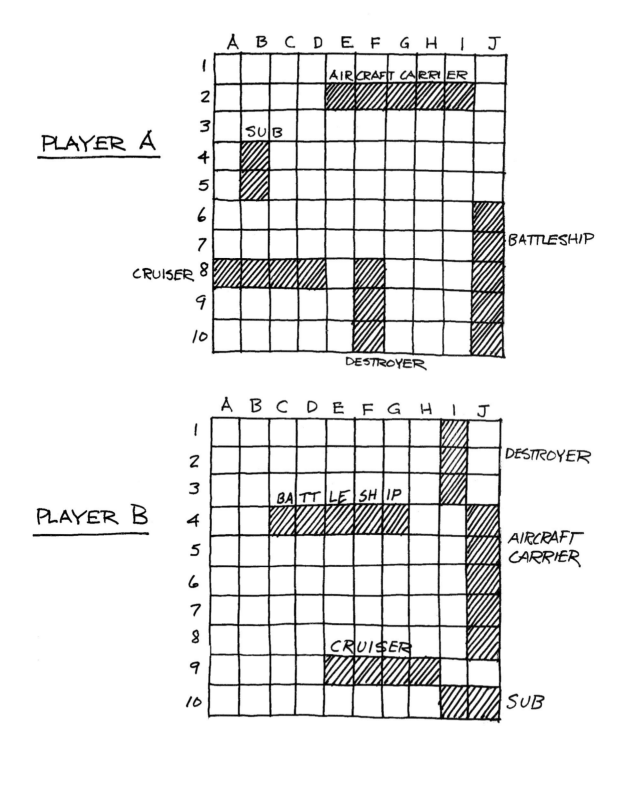

PLAYER A

PLAYER B

6. The second player then takes her turn, calling out a square she thinks might be part of one of her opponent's ships. No extra turn is earned for a hit.

7. Each player keeps track of his or her own guesses on the Shots grid, marking each hit with an *X*. Misses are marked down with a dot, so that the same square is not called out twice.

8. Once a player has hit all the squares occupied by a ship, he has sunk that ship. The first player to sink all of her opponent's ships is the winner.

Hint: If a player scores a hit, she should make her next guess in one of the squares next to the one she hit. This will tell her whether the ship has been placed horizontally or vertically, and therefore where her next guesses should be.

For a longer game, make a larger grid and add more ships.

MAGIC TRICKS

UNPOPPABLE BALLOON
Show the power of the magic word.

You will need:
- 1 balloon
- clear tape
- straight pin, safety pin, or sewing needle

1. Before you begin, blow up the balloon and stick a small piece of clear tape (about one inch long) onto it. Don't let anyone see you do this. Make sure not to get any fingerprints on the tape before you apply it and smooth out the tape after you've put it on the balloon to remove any wrinkles. The tape should be almost invisible.

2. Tell your friends that you know a magic word that will keep the balloon from popping. Show them the pin.

3. Say your magic word and quickly stick the pin into the taped part of your balloon. The balloon shouldn't pop.

4. Just to prove how powerful your magic word is, tell your friends that forgetting to say the word is disastrous. Pull out the pin, then stick it into some part of the balloon that is not taped.

5. When the balloon pops, it gives your trick a dramatic ending, while destroying any evidence of your tape trickery.

THE NEW HOUDINI
An "impossible" escape

You will need:

    2 pieces of string or rope (4 feet long each)
    1 door with 2 doorknobs

1. Tie loops into both ends of both pieces of string using strong double knots that won't slip. The loops should be big enough for you to put your hands into easily.

2. Put each loop of the first string on the doorknobs of an open door, as shown.

3. Put your right wrist through one of the loops on the second piece of string. Pass the other end of that piece through the opening created by the string that's hanging between the two doorknobs, then put your left wrist through the empty loop.

4. Show your friends how you are "handcuffed" to the door. Ask one of them if he or she can free you without taking the loops off of your wrists.

5. When they have all given up, explain that you are the new Houdini and can escape from anything. Take the middle of the string that is attached to the door and hold it together in a loop.

6. Push this loop through the handcuff on your right wrist, then pull the loop over your right hand.

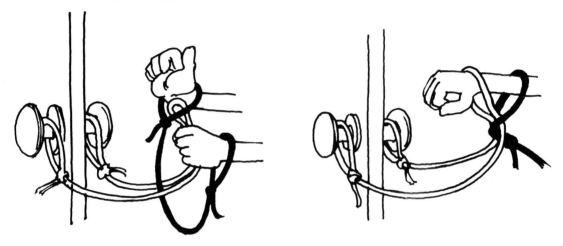

7. Pull away from the door, allowing the handcuff on your right hand to slide over the loop attached to the door. You're free!

MAGNETIC MONEY CLIPS
The force that brings the two clips together is you!

You will need:
   1 dollar bill
   2 metal paper clips

1. Explain to your friends that you have the power to magnetize the paper clips so that they will link themselves together in midair.

2. Fold the right side of the dollar bill over about a third of the way (George Washington's picture will be covered). Do not crease the fold. Clip the two layers of the bill together, with the top of the paper clip at the top of the bill. As you do this, explain that George Washington did this trick first, and since every dollar bill has his picture, it contains some of that same magic.

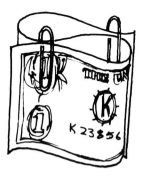

3. Turn the bill over and fold a third of the other side, still without creasing your fold. Slide the other paper clip onto the top of the bill, but clip only two layers together. Both of your paper clips should frame the number 1 that appears on the front and back of the dollar bill.

4. Hold the edges of the bill and pull them quickly but firmly apart, saying some patriotic magic words (such as, "By the dawn's early light") as you do.

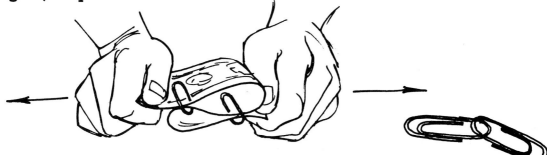

5. If you have clipped the bill properly, the clips will leap into the air and fall to the ground, attached to each other. Show the clips to your friends and be sure to thank George Washington.

For an extra twist, you can do the trick again, adding a rubber band that will also link up with the clips. Explain to your friends that you know a way to keep track of the magnetic clips, since they can fly off and get lost. After step 2, slip a rubber band around the dollar bill. The rubber band should be big enough to hang loosely on the bill. Finish clipping the bill as usual and pull apart the edges as before. Now your clips will be linked to each other and to the rubber band.

MIND READER
Guess the right animal every time.

You will need:
    paper
    pencil
    hat

1. Tear up a piece of paper into small slips. Eight or ten of them will do, but you can make as many as you like.

2. Hold one of the slips in your hand and ask a friend for the name of an animal. Write that name on the slip of paper, fold the slip in half, and put it into a hat.

3. Take another slip, ask for a different animal's name, and write again on the slip of paper. But this time, write the same animal as you did the first time. Don't let your friends see what you're writing. Fold the slip and drop it into the hat.

4. Continue to ask for more animal names, pretending each time to write the new name on another slip of paper. Each time, however, you will write the same animal name on the slip before folding it and dropping it into the hat.

5. When all the slips have been used, hold out the hat and ask one of your friends to pick one. Turn your head as they read the name to themselves.

6. Turn around and look like you're concentrating fiercely. Snap your fingers as though the answer has just come to you and tell them the name of the first animal. Because you've written that

name on all the slips, it will be the correct one, and your friends will think you're a mind reader.

7. Gather up the slips of paper before anyone can read the rest of them, explaining that the concentration of mind reading has given you a headache, and you can't read any more minds. Leave your friends to talk about your psychic abilities.

THE TALKING CARDS
Cards can't talk, but your friends will think they do!

You will need:
> 1 deck of cards

1. Before you begin this trick, put the four Jacks on top of a deck of cards. Don't let your friends know you did this.

2. Facing your audience, put the top four cards— the Jacks—face down separately on the table.

3. Deal out the rest of the cards into piles on these four cards. Not every pile has to have the same number of cards. In fact, the trick looks better if they're different sizes.

4. Turn around so you can't see the cards and tell your friends to look at the top card on each pile.

5. When they have done this, turn back around and gather up the cards. Put one pile on top of the next so that you have one deck again.

6. Take the top card off the deck and turn it over. "This one is easy," you should say. "It's already on the top. But it's going to tell me where the other three cards are." Hold the card up to your ear and nod thoughtfully, as though you are listening to the card.

7. With the face side up, fan out the rest of the deck in your hand to the right and look for each of the four Jacks. One Jack will be on the very bottom of the deck, and you can ignore it. The other three will be scattered throughout the pile, on top of the top cards from your pile.

8. As you find each of the other three Jacks, pull out the card to the right of it. These will be the cards from the top of each of the piles. Show each card to the first card you turned over, asking it, "Is this one of the cards?" It will be, of course, and your friends will be amazed at how well you can talk to a playing card.

STRING THINGS

IN THE BLINK OF AN EYE
Watch out or you'll miss it!

You will need:

 1 long piece of string or cord (about 2 feet) with the ends tied together

1. Hang a loop of string over four fingers on your left hand, as shown.

2. Close your pinkie, ring, and middle fingers over the loop. Your hand should look like this.

3. Use your right hand to wrap the string hanging down the back of your left hand around your index finger, and then take that string around the back of your thumb.

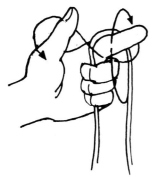

4. Tuck your thumb under the loop you just created on your index finger. Use your right hand if you need help making the loop bigger. Then pull your thumb back to its original position.

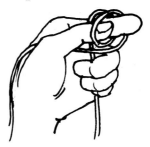

5. Pick up the long string that's hanging down against the outside of your thumb and pull it forward so it drapes over the string between your thumb and index finger.

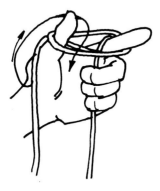

6. Release the string you've been holding with your three fingers and loop it behind your thumb.

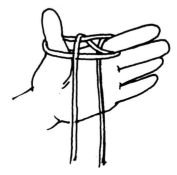

7. To make your eye blink, pull sideways on the loop that's hanging down. This will pull your thumb and index finger closer together. To open the eye, loosen your hold on the hanging loop and pull your finger and thumb apart.

For fun, you and a friend can each make this figure and put your blinking eyes together. Then try to make the pair of eyes blink in sync!

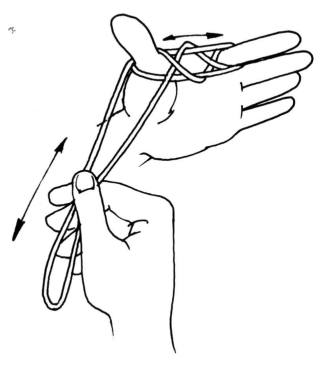

CAPTURE
Hold a hand hostage!

You will need:

1 long piece of string with the ends tied together

1. Take the loop of string and stretch it across your thumbs.

2. Pick up the far string with your pinkies.

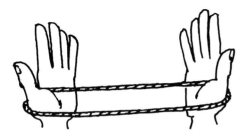

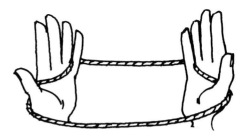

3. Pick up the string lying across the palm of your left hand, using your right index finger. Pull your hands apart as far as they will go.

4. Pick up the string lying across your right palm, using your left index finger. The string should be pulled from in between the loop you created in step 3.

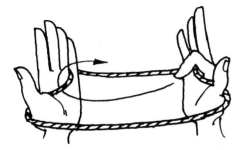

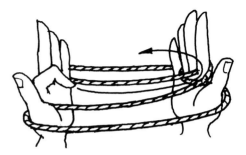

5. Pull your hands apart as far as they will go. Your hands should look like this.

6. Ask a volunteer to put his hand through the top of the middle loop of the figure.

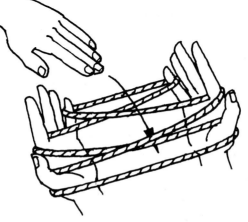

7. Drop the loops that are on your pinkies and index fingers. Pull your thumbs apart until the string is taut. You have "captured" your volunteer's hand!

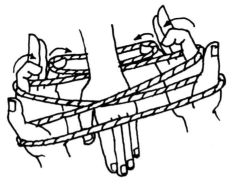

8. With your friend's wrist captured, repeat steps 2 through 5.

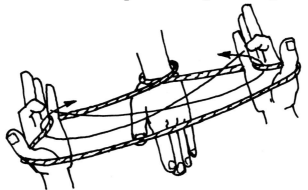

9. Ask your friend to put his wrist through the loop in the center of your new figure without removing his wrist from the string. This time he should come up through the bottom.

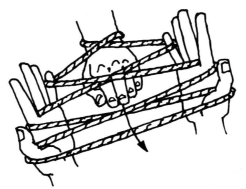

10. Again, drop the loops on your pinkies and index fingers. Your friend will be amazed to find that his hand has been released from his handcuff!

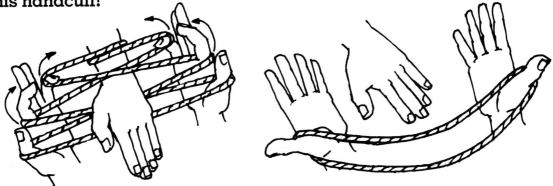

STRIPED FRIENDSHIP BRACELET
It looks hard, but it's knot!

You will need:

> 3 pieces of different-colored thread, 1 arm's length long each
>> Note: Embroidery thread works best
>
> safety pin
> scissors

1. Knot your threads together by laying out all three lengths in a row. Fold the strings in half, and then tie a knot in the end to create a loop, as shown. Spread the other ends of the threads out into a fan so that they are separated. It will be easier to work with your bracelet if you secure the knotted end to a pillow with a safety pin.

2. The thread on the far left will be thread A (the knotting thread), the thread to its right will be thread B, and so forth, through thread F on the far right.

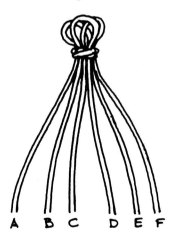

3. Take thread A in your right hand. Holding thread B in your left hand, loop thread A over thread B.

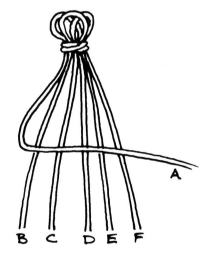

4. Then bring thread A under thread B, through the opening, and over thread A, making a loose knot, as shown. To tighten the knot, keep thread B tight and pull thread A outward to the top of the bracelet. It is very important that you keep thread B pulled downward firmly and do not tighten the knot by pulling outward with both threads.

5. With thread A, tie another knot on thread B in the same way, then put thread B to the left side.

6. Make two knots with thread A in the same way on threads C, D, E, and F, in that order. Be careful to keep your bracelet on the same side and don't let it flip over. These knots have made the first row in your bracelet, and the thread that began at the far left as thread A is now all the way on the far right.

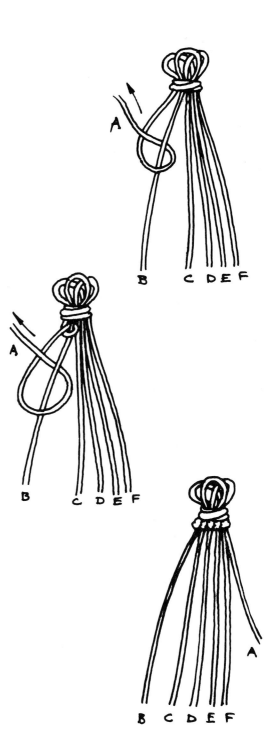

7. Now begin the second row by using thread B to tie two knots around threads C, D, E, F, and A, until thread B is on the far right. As you make each knot on the second row, pull the knot tight so that it is snug against the first row.

8. Continue making rows. The fourth row should be the same color stripe as the first row, and the color order will repeat itself as you work downward.

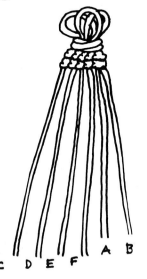

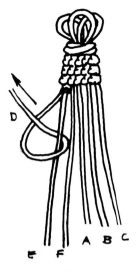

9. When the bracelet goes two-thirds of the way around your wrist, you are ready to braid the ends. You will make two braids of three threads apiece. Reletter the threads A through F, as they were at the beginning. Then take thread A and lay it over thread B.

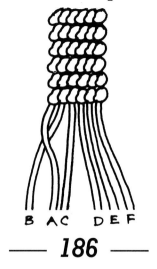

10. Lay thread C over thread A. The threads are now in B, C, A order.

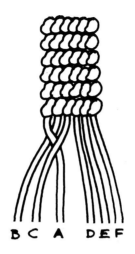

B C A D E F

11. Continue braiding in this way, tightening the braid as you go. When the braid is about 3 inches long, tie a knot in the end of the braid to finish it.

12. Now braid the other three threads, D, E, and F, the same way. Trim the threads, then tie the two braids through the loop in the other end. Your bracelet is done.

SPIRAL BRACELET
A thinner, easier model

You will need:

    4 different-colored threads, 1 arm's length long each
        Note: Embroidery thread works best
safety pin
scissors

1. Tie all of the ends of the thread together in a knot. Leave 3 to 4 inches above the knot so you will be able to tie the bracelet ends to each other when you've finished. It will be easier to work with your bracelet if you secure the knotted end to a pillow with a safety pin.

2. Choose one color to begin the spiral. The thread on the far left will be thread A, which you will tie around the other three threads.

3. To knot thread A around the other three threads, first make a small triangle by pulling thread A at an angle to the left, then bringing it over the other threads to the right.

4. Then loop thread A back under the threads to the left and finish the knot by bringing the tip of the thread back through the triangle and over thread A.

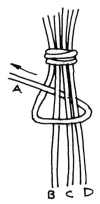

5. Tighten the knot by pulling thread A up to the top of the bracelet while holding the other three threads tight.

6. Tie about five more knots with thread A, noticing that the knots are moving to the right. If you begin with thread A on the right and make the small triangle on the right, the knots will travel to the left.

7. When thread A reaches the right side of your bracelet, wrap it under the bracelet so that it's on the left side of your bracelet again.

8. Continue making knots until you have three spirals, about twenty or twenty-five knots. Then pick up thread B and knot it around the other threads.

9. Continue making spirals and changing colors until your bracelet reaches around your wrist. Tie the loose ends together and cut any long threads that are left. Your spiral bracelet is finished!

ANSWERS

Page 143:

Each letter is represented by one number. A = 1, B = 2, all the way to Z = 26.

a. Yellow

b. Green

c. Red

d. Orange

e. Brown

Page 144:

1. Ten pounds. Two halves make a whole, so if the brick's weight is the sum of five pounds and half the total weight, the other half must also be five.

2. 987,654,321. Twice half of any number is that same number.

3. 43. One-half goes into 20 forty times, not ten.

4. If all but nine died, then nine sheep were left.

5. Zero. All those other numbers before it don't mean anything, because anything times zero is zero.

Page 145:

Answer these questions from memory, then go back to the picture to check your answers.

How many people are in the picture?

What three kinds of bikes are people riding?

What is the name of the moving company?

How many people are wearing hats?

How many wheels can you see on the moving truck?

What is the mover carrying out of the truck?

Page 146:

1. Doreen, A, air rifle

2. Janet, B, houseplant

3. Doug, D, candy

4. Alan, C, teddy bear

Page 147:

1. Terrence, C, Elvis

2. Brett, A, Howler

3. Jill, D, Tango

4. Courtney, B, Alfalfa

Page 148:

For the envelope, connect the lines in the following pattern: E to B to D to C to B to A to C to F to D to E to F. For the circle puzzle, start by connecting A to B; then take the upper curve from B to E; then to D; then take the upper curve to C; then draw a straight line to D; then take the lower curve to C; then draw a straight line to B; then take the lower curve to E; and finish by connecting E to F.

Page 149:

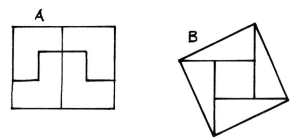

Page 150:

1. open bird's beak, closed bird's beak
2. double left window frame, single left window frame
3. five rows of shingles, four rows of shingles
4. two steps, three steps
5. rocking chair, four-legged chair
6. split roof window, whole roof window
7. three door windows, two door windows
8. nine apples in tree, eight apples plus one pear in tree
9. post behind hill, no post behind hill
10. all flies right side up, one fly upside down
11. different curtain patterns

Page 151:   **Page 152:**

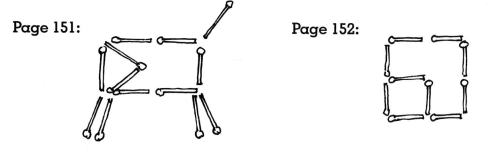

Page 153:

1. Fill the five-quart bottle, then fill up the three-quart bottle from it. That will leave two quarts in the five-quart bottle. Empty the three-quart bottle, then pour the remaining two quarts from the five-quart bottle into it. Fill the five-quart bottle again. Now you have two quarts in the three-quart bottle and five quarts in the five-quart bottle, for a total of exactly seven quarts.

2. One day. It doesn't matter how many half eggs each hen can lay, since each of the twenty-five hens can lay at least one egg in a day.